A Handbook ~~~ with a Loved One in the Hospital

> "24/7 OR DEAD is written by a non-medical person—a regular American—who experienced firsthand the devastating events of her spouse's life-threatening illness. Jari Holland Buck knows upfront and personal the best and worst that can happen in a modern U.S. hospital today."
> *Jane Murray, M.D., former Director of the Division of Education, American Academy of Family Physicians*

The fifth leading cause of death in American hospitals is medical mistakes. Church leaders who offer comfort and counsel to sick individuals and their families are frequently asked, "Is there anything else I can do?" The best answer any of us previously had was, "Pray." Now, we **can** and **must** do more to prevent our loved one from becoming part of the medical mistake death statistics.

24/7 or Dead is a guidebook that describes advocacy techniques on behalf of a hospitalized loved one. *24/7 or Dead* provides 14 practical suggestions illustrated by real life examples and checklists to ensure that even in emotionally charged situations, advocacy can be accomplished. This book also addresses personal care, without which advocacy is not possible. *24/7 or Dead* is designed to encourage and support family members in the process of reclaiming the "power of partnership" with the healthcare community.

This book is geared for the medically untrained family member who needs a step-by-step process for educating themselves and partnering with healthcare professionals to improve the health and comfort of the patient.

The early chapters deal with choices, the middle chapters with actions and the final chapters with results. Examples of the use or failure to use each step are illustrated, as are the consequences and results. The difficulty of advocating when resisted by healthcare providers is explored, as are the diverse responses to advocacy by the healthcare community. Legal issues are identified and sample legal documents are provided.

"It is my hope that *24/7 or Dead* will convert previously passive lay people into advocates and previously directive healthcare providers into partners. Mahatma Gandhi once said, 'Be the change you want to see in the world.' I had to become the change in order to help save my husband. Will you join me?"

Jari Holland Buck is a business consultant, trainer and medical layperson who spent eight and a-half months in four hospitals by the side of her critically ill husband. She dealt with thousands of doctors and nurses and almost daily crises. During her husband's six plus months on full life support, every organ in his body failed, some more than once. This book represents the lessons she learned and used in partnership with the medical community to produce a miracle, her husband's survival.

Jari's work has been recognized in International Who's Who of Entrepreneurs, Who's Who of American Women, Who's Who of the United States, Who's Who in America, Who's Who in Finance and Business, Who's Who of Business Executives and Who's Who of Emerging Leaders.

24/7 or Dead

A Handbook for Families with a Loved One in the Hospital

By

Jari Holland Buck

[signature]

http://www.24-7ordead.com

1663 Liberty Drive, Suite 200
Bloomington, Indiana 47403
(800) 839-8640
www.AuthorHouse.com

© 2006 Jari Holland Buck. All Rights Reserved.

No part of this book may be reproduced, stored in a retrieval system, or transmitted by any means without the written permission of the author.

First published by AuthorHouse 1/06/06

ISBN: 1-4208-5982-X (sc)
1-4259-1083-1 (e)

Library of Congress Control Number: 2005905075

Printed in the United States of America
Bloomington, Indiana

This book is printed on acid-free paper.

IMPORTANT NOTE TO READERS:
The suggestions in this book for patient advocacy are not meant to substitute for the advise of a licensed professional such as a doctor or a nurse. Rather, the intent and spirit of this book is to join in partnership with such professionals. It is essential to consult such professionals in any treatment offered by a hospital. The publisher and author expressly disclaim any liability for injuries resulting from use by readers of the methods contained in this book.

PERMISSIONS
Quotations in Chapters 1, 8 and 15 are reprinted with permission from Work, Rich with Ann Marie Goth: Awaken To The Healer Within, Mosinee, WI, 1995, pgs 23-24, 153. Copyrighted by Rich Work.

10 Warning Signs of Caregiver Stress in Chapter 16 is reprinted with permission from the Alzheimer's Association, copyright 1995.

A Consumer Fact Sheet: The Role of the Patient Advocate in the Appendix is reprinted with permission from the National Patient Safety Foundation (NPSF), © 2003.

The Fearless Caregiver Manifesto in the Appendix is reprinted with permission from Barg, Gary, Editor and Publisher of Today's Caregiver Magazine and caregiver.com: The Fearless Caregiver, How to Get the Best Care for Your Loved One and Still Have A Life of Your Own, Sterling, VA, October 15, 2001. Copyrighted by Capital Books.

Wong-Baker FACES Pain Rating Scale in the Appendix is reprinted with permission from Wong D.L., Hockenberry-Eaton M., Wilson D., Winkelstein M.L., Schwartz P.: Wong's Essentials of Pediatric Nursing, ed. 6, St. Louis, 2001, p. 1301. Copyrighted by Mosby, Inc.

Sample Patient Rights Statement in the Appendix is reprinted with permission from the author.

Sample Medical Information and Privacy Statement in the Appendix is reprinted with permission from the author.

This book is dedicated to my beloved husband, Bill Buck, who has always given me a reason to live and love.

I also gratefully acknowledge the following healthcare providers, friends and family who played a crucial role in the care and feeding (in the truest sense of the word) of my husband's body and my spirit:

Dorothy Buck
Rebecca Davis, R.N.
Gigi Fergus, R.N.
Sandy Ferguson, R.N.
Ruth Theis, R.N.
Tim Malloy, R.N.
Lee Gorcos, R.R.T.
Pam Sagoo, R.R.T.
My friend, Jean, Reiki Practitioner
Mitzi McFatrich, Cranial Sacral Specialist
Randal Brown, M.D.
Richard Huseman, M.D.
Larry Botts, M.D.
James H. Thomas, M.D., R.V.T.
Ben Cowley, M.D.
Franz Winklhofer, M.D.
Steve Simpson, M.D.
Ira Silverman, M.D.
Holly Fritch Kirby, M.D.
Jane Murray, M.D.
Pat Bates, MSL- CCC-SLP
Skip Fannen, J.D.
Susan, Ronald, Jason and Jeffrey Miller
Janice Ubben
Pat Nasko Smith
Kevin Kelly
Carin Goodemote
Steve Smith
Curt Starnes, J.D.
Len Chmelka
The Employees of Universal Underwriters Group
The Prayer Circle - Country Club United Methodist Church

TABLE OF CONTENTS

A Doctor's Perspective on Advocacy ix

A Patient's Perspective on Advocacy xiii

An Advocate's Perspective on Advocacy xvii

CHAPTER 1 Read Me First, Read Me Often 1

CHAPTER 2 One Day, After Lunch 13

CHAPTER 3 Take Care of Yourself 37

CHAPTER 4 Choose Your Hospital with Awareness 55

CHAPTER 5 Pick the Days of Your Stay Carefully 77

CHAPTER 6 Execute a Durable Medical Power of Attorney, a Living Will and a Power of Attorney 85

CHAPTER 7 Read and Use the Patient Rights Statement 95

CHAPTER 8 Assume Your Loved One Can Hear Everything So Phrase Everything in the Positive 117

CHAPTER 9 Educate Yourself 123

CHAPTER 10 Ask About Every Medication, Injection or Intravenous Solution Used or Denied in Treatment. 131

CHAPTER 11 Understand Every Procedure Used or Denied in Treatment 141

CHAPTER 12 Keep Track of All Supplies and Other Duplicated or Unwarranted Services Used in Treatment 161

CHAPTER 13 Stay in the Room 24/7 165

CHAPTER 14 Pray 169

CHAPTER 15 Surrender 173

CHAPTER 16 Take Care of Yourself 181

Appendix	189
A Consumer Fact Sheet	190
The Fearless Caregiver Manifesto	195
Pain Assessment Tool	197
Sample Durable Power of Attorney – Healthcare	198
Sample Living Will	200
Sample Power of Attorney	202
Sample Patient Rights Statement	204
Sample Medical Information and Privacy Statement	211
Actively Participate in the Billing/Payment Process	229
Additional Resources	237

A Doctor's Perspective on Advocacy

24/7 or Dead: A Handbook for Families with a Loved One in the Hospital is written by a non-medical person—a regular American—who experienced firsthand the devastating events of her spouse's life-threatening illness. Jari Holland Buck knows upfront and personal the best and worst that can happen in a modern U.S. hospital today.

Her husband, Bill, was stricken suddenly with severe pancreatitis, which rapidly progressed to multiple organ failure, severe infection, seizures and about every possible step toward death that any healthcare professional might imagine.

After eight and a-half months in the hospital—over six months of that time in ICUs on full life support—Bill is miraculously alive, walking and recovering slowly from multiple long-term assaults on his system. That he is alive at all is a tribute to some of the wonders of modern medicine. But having been involved peripherally in Bill's hospital care and directly in Jari's journey with him, I can honestly say his survival is mostly due to Jari's committed presence. Her attention to detail, willingness to question nurses, doctors and therapists and insistence that her involvement in and partnering with the healthcare team be taken seriously were key factors in his being alive today. She was tough. She asked hard questions. She insisted upon being informed of all test results. I imagine she irritated some of the healthcare providers working so hard to keep Bill alive. But she was right to do so.

She was at Bill's side virtually every minute and throughout all of his acute care, and it was good she was. She picked up vital sign irregularities that could have led to death, despite continuous electronic monitoring. She collated information and asked probing questions. She sought the best care possible for Bill's complex and unique situation. When she did not get answers that made sense to her, she insisted on more information, more explanation and even a change of facilities and doctors. If she had not done these things, Bill surely would have died.

This book could not have been written by anyone other than a family member who was determined to do the very best for a loved one. Healthcare professionals—unless they have been through such an intense and personal experience—cannot know the detail and the emotion that occurs on the other side of the nurse's station.

As a doctor, I know I care about my patients. I know I always want to do the very best I can to help them. But there is no way I will ever be as diligent about every one of my patients as they themselves and their family will be. Thus, a partnership! If we doctors, nurses, therapists and others in healthcare will take to heart Jari's and Bill's experiences and success, we can add an absolutely crucial dimension to our care of patients. We can never know everything, be aware of everything or track every detail all of the time. We need help. Families and loved ones can truly help us in our journey to assist the lifesaving and healing processes to which we devote our lives. Let us invite them onto the healthcare team.

Jane Murray, M.D.
Sastun Center of Integrative Healthcare
Mission, Kansas

Former Director of the Division of Education
American Academy of Family Physicians

Past Chair of the Department of Family Medicine
University of Kansas Medical Center

A Patient's Perspective on Advocacy

A View from the Bed

My life changed forever the day my pancreas blew up. Although I am reasonably certain no doctor in the world would describe my disease in this fashion, that is how I think about it. I was an exercise fanatic and convinced that if I worked out at least three times per week, I would be disease-proof. Obviously, that was a case of flawed thinking. *Physically*, I will never be whole again.

Before becoming disabled, I was rehabbing our home, building a B&O HO scale railroad model and filling the role of Chief Legal Counsel for an insurance company. My work frequently brought me in contact with doctors who, I believed, were entitled to obedience and respect on a nearly religious level. I now believe challenging a doctor could save your life. *Mentally*, I discovered the flaw in blind faith.

Prior to my illness, I did not understand how people could pray to a being I couldn't see, hear, touch, taste, or smell. I now recognize prayer helped keep me alive. *Spiritually*, I can no longer dispute the power of joined hearts and minds in a quest for a miracle. I am one of those miracles!

I visited my surgeon last week for the first time in more than a year. I thanked him for saving my life. What was his response? "Your wife was the one who kept you alive." Once again my flawed thinking brought me up short. *Emotionally*, I live in debt and gratitude.

On every plane of my very existence, my disease caused me to rethink suppositions and beliefs that I had carried with me throughout my life. The single most important shift I experienced occurred when I observed and benefited from a form of fierce and protective energy wielded by my wife. Although sometimes embarrassing, sometimes amazing, sometimes humbling, sometimes critical, I simply cannot deny the power of a dedicated, single-minded and caring advocate. I am fully convinced Jari is the reason I'm still here. Advocacy saved my life and my marriage, and I would not have it any other way.

I am told Jari did a great deal of advocacy for me before I woke up, but I didn't see or hear her in action until the time I came to. My first conscious thought was, "Oh my God, I've been in a car wreck." I panicked and got really scared. Following an explanation of my "dance with death," I began to watch the medical care providers, trying to determine whether I was being properly cared for.

What really got my attention was Jari. I noticed that doctors and other staff took Jari quite seriously, accepting her advice and even altering the course of care when she would point out things that were done or ordered that might have had a negative effect on me. She even got these busy professionals to pay attention to little things like my chapped lips and dry eyes.

My fondest memory of Jari's role and action was a phrase I overheard from just outside my room door, "If you think you've seen trouble before, you ain't seen nothin' yet!" (Yeah, Jari!) Ordinarily, a family member would accept care plans and actions by medical staff without question or complaint. Jari did not respond that way, *ever*, as far as I can tell. God bless her for that attitude!

There were very tough times when Jari was needed to be the cool head in the group. On one occasion during a holiday, I needed an immediate consultation, but a staff person refused to call an M.D. at his home "because he was entitled to time with his family, too." Jari kicked some serious butt that day, and I got what I needed. Perhaps I even got to stay alive because she had the guts to call protocol into question. Nice talk and good manners don't save lives. As an attorney, I am professionally trained to speak up on behalf of another, but I learned some lessons from Jari.

Know what ails your loved one, in detail. Use the Internet to get the information that is there for the picking. You can even begin to talk just like a "real doctor" and be compellingly persuasive in the process. My wife got the equivalent of a Ph.D. in medicine through her extensive self-study of all my conditions. Also, if there is a way to feel in touch and in balance while your loved one battles for his life, it is through such self-study and challenge to the status quo. I believe this is the one time in your life to make sure you are heard, even though the listener may not want to hear what you have to say. Kick butt and don't try to make friends. You and your loved one are in a pitched battle to make sure that life and health prevail.

William C. Buck, J.D.
The patient

An Advocate's Perspective on Advocacy

Here is the test to find whether your mission on Earth is finished: if you're alive, it isn't.
—Richard Bach

The very best place for a critically ill patient to be is in the hospital. The very worst place for a critically ill patient to be is in the hospital.

It is a double bind of the worst kind, especially for family members of that critically ill patient. There are many reasons why hospitals have become such frightening places. Look at the economic factors:

- Healthcare will be reeling from the influx of 76–78 million baby boomers over the next 20 years.

- In less than 20 years, 35 percent of the population will be age 50 or older.

- Today, out-of-pocket healthcare costs average 19 percent of income for persons age 65 and over in the United States. The percentage is even higher for those with low incomes. Those without Medicaid spend almost HALF of their total income on healthcare.

Economics aside, the most distressing reason for poor healthcare is the loss of the concept of care. The *American Heritage Dictionary of the English Language* defines care as "attentive assistance or treatment to those in need." Today, providing medical services to consumers is a business—a business that to the uneducated and the educated alike appears to care not at all about the human factors involved in the care and feeding of the body and the spirit.

My husband was hospitalized for eight and a-half months, six of which were in intensive care and on life support. My motivation in sharing our experience is not driven by a desire to lambaste managed care providers or to indict medical insurance companies. Anyone who remembers how medical treatment was provided ten or twenty years ago cannot be anything but disappointed with the services provided today. The healthcare system in the United States today is badly broken and I, as a consumer, do not know how to fix it.

Given the critical healthcare environment today, there are extreme risks for every patient. This is due to the low level of care. Hospitals are notoriously understaffed, in the spirit of cost containment. I have personally witnessed a 1:16 ratio of nurses to patients. How can any human being, even with the best intentions, provide anything other than the very basics of physical care when they have sixteen patients? For care partners (formerly known as nurse's aides) there can be an even higher ratio.

A study conducted by researchers at the University of Pennsylvania involving 232,000 surgical patients at 168 hospitals concluded that a patient's overall risk of death rose roughly 7 percent for each additional patient above four for whom a nurse was assigned to care. Translated, that meant on the day my husband experienced a 1:16 nurse-to-patient ratio, he was 84 percent more likely to die!

The Harvard School of Public Health conducted a study of 6 million patients and found that patients in hospitals with lower numbers of registered nurses were more likely to suffer complications and die from those treatable complications.

Consider these startling facts.

- Fewer women are entering nursing.
- Only 5.4 percent of nurses are men.
- Twenty percent of all licensed registered nurses have left active nursing.
- Nursing schools turned away 5,900 qualified applicants in 2000.
- There are 11,500 fewer students in nursing schools today than in 1995.
- If unchecked, hospital nursing vacancies will rise to nearly 400,000 by 2020, leaving nearly one in five positions unfilled.
- Last year, in surveys of practicing nurses, four of ten reported being dissatisfied with their work. More than half said they would not recommend nursing as a career. One of five planned to leave their current job within one year.

Clearly, things are NOT getting better. And, as Henry Miller states, *"Everything we shut our eyes to, everything we run away from, everything we deny, denigrate, or despise, serves to defeat us in the end."*

What about doctors? Doctors are notoriously overworked because the only way they cover their expenses is to take on additional patients. Why? Because insurance carriers have created the concept of preferred providers, thereby enabling them to heavily discount the doctor's fees (up to 50 percent). The result is that doctors need to treat as many as twice the number of patients they previously treated to achieve the same financial return. Additionally, Medicare is not keeping up with the rising cost of healthcare, leading many doctors to refuse to treat Medicare patients.

And then there are the hospital administrators, who are driven by the numbers as surely as any CEO in the private sector.

So, what can we as healthcare consumers do? Changing the system feels overwhelming and impossible. So, let's assume the status quo and focus on protecting our loved ones and ourselves. We can do this by taking personal responsibility for avoiding the extreme risks to the patient due to the low level of care. How do we do this? By providing the care ourselves—real care twenty-four hours a day, seven days a week.

What does this look like? This book presents a fairly painful illustration of what patient care is truly about. I strongly recommend you become a patient advocate, a position supported by AARP (formerly known as the American Association of

Retired Persons) and the National Patient Safety Foundation (NPSF®). NPSF® is an organization committed to making patient safety a national priority. An independent, nonprofit research and education organization regarding the role of patient advocates, it was founded in 1996 by the American Medical Association, CNA/HealthPro and 3M with contributions from Schering-Plough. NPSF® publishes a consumer fact sheet, *The Role of the Patient Advocate*, which they have generously allowed me to include in the Appendix.

I am not advocating that we make patients out of ourselves by monitoring and caring ourselves into exhaustion. I am advocating very strongly for the full-time presence of a family member for every patient in a hospital. I had no previous experience doing this, and certainly do not know all the right things to do. I did, however, learn some very important lessons about what it took to keep my husband alive.

During my attempts to get this book to the market, many publishers told me that although I had good ideas, my message should be carried by a healthcare professional, such as a doctor or a nurse. I could not accept that answer. Through my organizational consulting practice, I have learned that individuals within a system, even when they hate the system, are reluctant to change it. At least in the here and now, those within a system know how to operate and respond. Anything new requires a new behavior. Learning new behaviors takes effort, something of which most healthcare workers have little to spare after the stress and workload of their daily existence. Although most healthcare workers may agree in principle with what I recommend, it **will** and did require them to change their behavior when I practiced my form of advocacy.

Change agents cannot operate from inside an organization. I know. I was one in my former professional life, and the system chewed me up and spit me out. I discovered the cost of advocating change from the inside was very high, up to and including the loss of my job. This price is too high for anyone in the business of saving lives. There are not enough of you, and we cannot afford to lose any more of you. Let me carry the message through this book.

And what is my message? **Without the full-time presence of a family member for every patient in a hospital, I believe there is a very good chance mistakes will be made. Some of those mistakes could cost your loved one his or her life.**

Do you want to risk a mistake being perpetrated upon your family member? Do you want to take the risk for yourself? If this risk seems unacceptable to you, join me as an advocate or a "pain in the ass family member" as some of the medical professionals will call you. Remember, we do this for love.

Jari Holland Buck
The advocate

To laugh is to risk appearing the fool.
To weep is to risk appearing sentimental.
To reach out for another is to risk involvement.
To expose feelings is to risk exposing your true self.
To place your ideas, your dreams, before a crowd is to risk their loss.
To love is to risk not being loved in return. To live is to risk dying.
To hope is to risk despair. To try is to risk failure.
But risks must be taken,
because the greatest hazard in life is to risk nothing.
The person who risks nothing, does nothing, has nothing and is nothing.
They may avoid suffering and sorrow,
but they cannot learn, feel, change, grow, love, live.
Only a person who risks is free.

—Author Unknown

CHAPTER 1
Read Me First, Read Me Often

You and I —
We meet as strangers,
each carrying a mystery
within us.
I cannot say who you are.
I may never know you completely.
But I trust that you are a person in your own right,
possessed of a beauty and value that are the Earth's richest
treasures.

So I make this promise to you:
I will impose no identities upon you,
but will invite you to become yourself
without shame or fear.
I will hold open a space for you
in the world
and allow your right to fill it with authentic vocation and
purpose.
For as long as your search takes, you have my loyalty.

—Author Unknown

Things happen for a reason. If you have found your way to this book, it is likely that you or a loved one are already in the hospital or are facing hospitalization in the near future. I don't know about you, but my attention span while sitting with my husband in the hospital was terrible. I was so distracted by the activity and so frightened by the noises I didn't understand that I could hardly stay in my body. That's why this chapter exists.

Recognizing you may be feeling like I did, this chapter tells you what you need to do to ensure that you or your loved one get the care you need and deserve. If you want the whys, wherefores, and examples of possible problems, the following chapters explain each recommendation, one at a time.

Here's how to use the information in this book:

- Read each recommendation.

- Decide which recommendations relate to your situation. For example, "Choose Your Hospital with Awarness" may not relate if you are already hospitalized or have limited options because of your geography, insurance requirements, or financial resources.

- Pick one of the recommendations and try it. Don't try to do all of them at one time. You will overwhelm yourself, lose confidence, **and** you could compromise your working relationship with the nurse or care provider. It took me over three months to figure this stuff out and then, when we ended up back in Intensive Care four weeks later, I had forgotten some of it. Take your time.

- Have confidence in yourself. **You can do this!** Remember, you are learning a brand-new language and brand-new skills. Take your time. Ask questions over and over until you understand. Take notes. Be gentle with yourself. Anything you can confront, you can handle.

- When you have implemented one of the recommendations, add another one. I have sequenced them in the order I believe will be most helpful to you and your loved one. However, if you want to tackle them in a different order, **do it!** The issue is not the order in which you implement but that you implement those recommendations that are helpful and relevant to your situation.

- At the end of several chapters, I have created checklists to assist you in implementation. I also left blank spaces for you to add your own personal needs related to each recommendation. If the checklists are helpful, use them. If not, do the recommendation your own way. Although I had a chance to implement each of these recommendations over a long period of time, by no means do I have a corner on the best way to do things for you. Frankly, I don't even have a corner on the best way to do things for myself sometimes!

- The point is not planning and control, measurable goals and clear pathways. The point is having clarity of values, learning to listen to yourself, risking action when control isn't possible. The point is focusing on what can be and must be, not on loss. And, most of all, keep your eyes and heart open. In the midst of it all, there will be moments of exquisite joy.

> *"Come to the edge," He said.*
> *They said: "We are afraid."*
> *"Come to the edge," He said.*
> *They came.*
> *He pushed them, and they flew.*
>
> —Guillaume Apollinaire

RECOMMENDATIONS

1. **TAKE CARE OF YOURSELF.** You are of no value to your loved one if you go down for the count. Sacrificing your own health for another is not what anyone who loves us would want us to do.

2. **CHOOSE YOUR HOSPITAL WITH AWARENESS.** Under populated hospitals offer far more care, at the

expense of far less doctor presence. Over populated hospitals offer far more doctor presence, at the expense of care. I've never found an appropriately populated hospital. Which is more important for your loved one – care or doctor's presence?

3. **PICK THE DAYS OF YOUR STAY CAREFULLY.** Nothing happens in hospitals on nights, weekends and holidays. Often, that includes the conduct of important procedures. Even hospitals with an appropriate doctor presence will be substandard on nights, weekends and holidays. Particularly on holidays, the least experienced staff will often provide care because those with seniority (experience) will bid for the time off. Try for Monday admission.

4. **EXECUTE A DURABLE MEDICAL POWER OF ATTORNEY, A LIVING WILL AND A POWER OF ATTORNEY.** No one can tell you what is going to happen and this is especially true when you are messing with the human body. No two bodies are the same. The same procedure can go perfectly 200 times and the 201st time, everything can go wrong.

5. **READ AND USE THE PATIENT RIGHTS STATEMENT.** Repeat it back to the hospital and

healtcare providers anytime they resist your questions or involvement. This is particularly true when you have Durable Medical Power of Attorney. Ask what the rules are and challenge any that don't make sense to you.

6. **ASSUME THAT YOUR LOVED ONE CAN HEAR EVERYTHING SO PHRASE EVERYTHING IN THE POSITIVE.** We are told that people in a coma can hear what we say, even if they cannot respond. Having an upsetting conversation with doctors or family members in the presence of your loved one, even when they are heavily sedated, can have extremely negative consequences. The universe (God) is always attentive to our requests. The universe (God) listens and responds to our requests. The universe (God) doesn't understand statements made in the negative. "Heal my husband" is a clear request. "Don't let my husband get sicker" is heard as "Let my husband get sicker." State everything in the positive.

7. **EDUCATE YOURSELF.** Learn everything you can about the illness, disease or injury being treated and about the equipment being used to provide treatment. The more you know, the more you can help the healthcare providers, even when they do not want your help. Rule #1 - equipment = tool. Use of equipment

Read Me First, Read Me Often

has dramatically improved health "care" in the last 20 years. However, many health "care" professionals rely so heavily on equipment, they fail to look at the patient. Rule #2—when in doubt, look at the patient.

8. **ASK ABOUT EVERY MEDICATION, INJECTION OR INTRAVENOUS SOLUTION USED OR DENIED IN TREATMENT.** Each medication has side effects, as television commercials have so pointedly illustrated.

9. **UNDERSTAND EVERY PROCEDURE USED OR DENIED IN TREATMENT.** Use the five "W's" to learn as much as you can from the doctors. Ask them:
   - *Who?*
   - *What?*
   - *When?*
   - *Where?*
   - *Why?*

10. **KEEP TRACK OF ALL SUPPLIES AND OTHER DUPLICATED OR UNWARRANTED SERVICES USED IN TREATMENT.** Refuse to pay for duplicate or unnecessary supplies and services. As you accumulate

supplies, post signs in the room to look in specified drawers/places for usable supplies.

11. **STAY IN THE ROOM 24/7.** This means twenty-four hours a day, seven days a week. You are the guardian. Maintain your post or pass it to someone else. This is especially true in Intensive Care. A-W-O-L could mean D-E-A-D.

12. **PRAY.**

13. **SURRENDER.** There is nothing like a serious illness to remind us how powerless we really are. In Alcoholics Anonymous, the First Step reads, *"Made a decision to turn my will and my life over to the care of God, as I understood Him."* This is surrender. You are responsible for the input. You are not responsible for the outcome.

14. **TAKE CARE OF YOURSELF.** You are of no value to your loved one if you go down for the count. Sacrificing your own health for another is not what anyone who loves us would want us to do.

According to Rollo May, *"Only the truth that is experienced at all levels of being has the power to change the human being."* Be prepared to be personally changed by what you are about to read and experience. To resist the change is to live

Read Me First, Read Me Often

in a healthcare world that no longer exists. Doctors, nurses, and other healthcare providers have feet of clay, even when coupled with the best intentions. Lest that clay cover you or your loved one's grave prematurely, you **must** act as if you or a loved one's life depends on 24/7 attention, **even if you do not believe it yet**.

Rich Work in his book, *Awaken to the Healer Within*, states,

> *If I can keep you in these* **Laws**,
> *If I can keep you in these* **Fears**,
> *If I can keep you in this* **Power**,
> *If I can keep you from* **Loving** *yourself* –
> *Just one of these – I can* **control** *you.*
> *All of them – I can* **own** *you.*
> —Reprinted with permission

You cannot allow someone else to make the healthcare decisions for you or another! You must act as a partner.

To do that, join me, another layperson like you, in:

> *Learning the* **Laws**,
> *Working through the* **Fears**,
> *Recognizing the* **Power** *of partnership*,
> **Loving** *yourself and your family*,
> *Ensuring you* **control** *decisions about your body*,
> *And* **owning** *your desire for health, happiness and life!*

I know that I was afraid, at times, to speak up. Busy care providers sometimes had a way of making me feel like I was bothering them or that I was "less than worthy" to ask questions. I was emboldened by an Eleanor Roosevelt quote I discovered, *"There is no more liberating, no more exhilarating experience than to determine one's position, state it bravely and then act boldly. Action creates its own courage; and courage is as contagious as fear."* And God knows, there was plenty of fear. I needed another compelling emotion to salve my heart.

This is a journey none of us take by choice. Both my husband and I, for different reasons, ran away from death. I buried seven family members and friends in five years during my childhood. He was an attorney who couldn't stand the smell of lilies because it reminded him of funerals. He refused to execute a will or any healthcare directives because he "didn't want to think about it"—the "it" being death. And, he lived with the belief that if he worked out three times a week, he could avoid death. He described himself as "bullet proof." I laugh in retrospect when I think of this match made out of "death aversion." By running away from it, we became a powerful magnet for death and it found us, hiding in the dark of my memories and his denial. For death we did experience, as nothing will ever be the same again.

Your journey through pain and illness to recovery will be different than ours. I would not expect you to accept what I am recommending without "credentialing" myself as an advocate.

Read Me First, Read Me Often

If you have the time, turn the page to learn more about the journey my husband, the patient, and I, the advocate, took through catastrophic illness to recovery. If you do not have time, or if illness/injury pressures require immediate action, your next step is to select a recommendation and begin.

Godspeed in your endeavor!

CHAPTER 2
One Day, After Lunch

God does not send us despair in order to kill us;
He sends it in order to awaken us to new life.

—Hermann Hesse, *Reflections*

I am usually so pigheaded that unless I experience something for myself, it is not real to me. I assume others live life the same way. However, I have found that stories, especially real-life stories, can make a difference. So, here is our story. Believe me when I say we have been there.

One day, after lunch and following a productive thrice-weekly session at the local health club, my husband, Bill, returned to work, munching on a tuna-salad sandwich. About thirty minutes later, he walked into his friend Skip's office and asked for a Rolaids, complaining of a stomachache. Thirty minutes after that, he collapsed on the floor in excruciating pain; paramedics were summoned.

I am told the pain of acute pancreatitis is comparable to childbirth, but I get ahead of myself…

Following the 911 call, Skip called me. I am a consultant and work from home. On that particular day, I was working on an intense analysis of employee interview data and, frankly, had not even showered or dressed. I was still in my pajamas from the previous night. The date was October 23, 2000, a day I will never forget, as it marked the commencement of a trip into hell that I feared we would never survive.

It was approximately 2:10 PM when I got Skip's call. He told me not to panic, but wanted me to know the paramedics were transporting Bill to a hospital close by their office. Because this was an emergency situation, Bill was taken to the hospital closest to his workplace. Bill had five of the signs of a medical emergency, as defined by the American College of Emergency Physicians:

1. *Difficulty in breathing or shortness of breath*
2. *Chest or abdominal pain or pressure*
3. *Fainting*
4. *Sudden dizziness*
5. *Any sudden, severe pain*

Although Bill was in severe pain, he was conscious and talking upon being loaded into the ambulance. Skip told me Bill had asked him not to call me, because he didn't want to worry me. This response came from Bill's knowledge of the numerous sudden deaths that had occurred in my family during my childhood and my terror of a repeat episode. Skip obviously ignored this request and called me anyway.

I remember thinking this could not be that serious if Bill was still conscious, so I finished the thought I had been working on before Skip's call and saved the file. Boy, was I wrong!

At 2:18 PM, I showered, threw on some clothes and drove quickly to meet Skip and another of Bill's colleagues in front of his office. Since I did not know where Bill had been taken, I followed them in my car to the hospital. As I came to expect, the hospital required me to provide insurance information before I was allowed access to my husband.

Bill was sitting on an emergency room bed, doubled over with terrible pain. They X-rayed his abdomen, drew blood, and did a CT scan, followed by placing a tube down his throat. This was designed to drain and remove all the contents from his stomach. They promised relief of pain upon completing this procedure, but relief was not forthcoming.

The Emergency Room (ER) doctor frequently stopped by to speak with us, and informed us he had asked for a consultation from a specialist. When the specialist arrived, he asked me (and Bill, who could not speak through the pain) how much alcohol Bill typically consumed. I replied he was not a drinker. The doctor did not believe me and repeated the question. I replied, "About six beers in a banner year." He then asked me if I knew for certain, adding that many drunks are good at hiding their drinking.

Having previously been married to an alcoholic, I was clearly aware of this! After divorce and more than ten years of therapy and recovery support groups, believe me, this was something I had verified before ever considering a relationship with Bill some fourteen years earlier. At this point, my patience ran out for the first of several hundred times to come. I moved to about an inch from the doctor's face, stating forcefully that I knew for a fact Bill was not a closet drinker. I also emphasized I had now answered his question for the third and last time and we were **not** going to discuss it again! Little did I know I would have this type of exchange thirty-one times over the course of Bill's illness and hospital stay, as a result of alcoholism being the number one cause of his disease.

That doctor finally apologized, explaining Bill had acute pancreatitis and that he would be hospitalized for several days. Treatment would include denial of food and water until his pancreas calmed down. (I later learned all the medical community knows to do for this disease is to maintain the patient while the disease takes it course.) The hospital admitted Bill to the Intensive Care Unit, hooked him up to several monitors, and provided a morphine pump for him to self-administer pain medication.

One of the monitors to which Bill was connected measured how much oxygen was getting to his body. When the oxygen level was too low, an alarm would sound. I stayed in Bill's hospital room that night and I would guess the alarm went off forty times. In spite of my coaching him to breathe deeply, he was clearly not getting sufficient oxygen. The next morning, approximately fifteen hours after admission, the same specialist told me we needed to temporarily place Bill on a ventilator (a machine that forcibly delivers humidified air under pressure to a patient's lungs) to ensure he would get enough air. This "temporary" solution lasted six months.

Bill and I both said, "I love you," and a nurse asked me to leave the room as the process could be "upsetting" for family members to watch. Bill was anesthetized into unconsciousness so the tube placed down his throat and attached to the ventilator would not be problematic. The doctors were still advising me a five to seven-day stay was probable.

Over the course of the next week, Bill's condition continued to deteriorate. His breathing, even on the ventilator, grew so bad that when the staff had to transport him down one floor for tests, he would "desaturate" (his oxygen consumption would fall well below acceptable levels).

Nurses drew blood daily, and sometimes more frequently, to determine what was going on metabolically. More and more lines were placed into my unconscious husband—lines to deliver medicine I did not understand, as well as food supplements, since he was unconscious.

In those early days, my focus was on what had caused this to happen to a perfectly healthy human being. My brother-in-law researched acute pancreatitis on the Internet, and my sister delivered the printed results daily when she visited. During his eight months of hospitalization, we explored and discounted every causal agent of his disease and, to this day, Bill is one of the fifteen percent of documented, unknown cause (idiopathic) acute pancreatitis patients.

Skip and Bill's boss came to the hospital daily and sat with me for hours on end. Bill's employer dispatched the company jet to Florida to pick up his mother and bring her here; they also paid for his kids to come on a commercial carrier. They even covered the cost of all of their hotel expenses. I came to understand that they (and many others) did not expect him to survive.

Bill's prognosis continued to deteriorate. He "coded" (short for Code Blue, the special response code for a heart or breathing stoppage) for the first of four times during week number two. His ventilator tube got plugged with the thick mucus he was producing and he stopped breathing. Thanks to the rapid response of his nurse and the coordinated efforts of his respiratory therapist, he survived.

The doctors were now saying it looked like he might have ARDS (Adult Respiratory Distress Syndrome), so I began researching ARDS. One doctor went so far as to say he thought Bill might also have congestive heart failure, so I researched that, too.

During the third week, Bill experienced his first of thirteen episodes of sepsis (a blood infection usually caused by an infection in one of the lines). Over the course of four hours, his blood pressure dropped repeatedly to 60/30, and we could not get it to more than 80/40 for very short periods of time. The nursing staff administered a series of drugs called pressors that are designed to elevate blood pressure, yet his pressure still hovered at a death-like level.

When they started the third pressor called Levophed ("Levo" for short), the nurses were considerate enough to withhold the informal remarks that typically accompany Levo—"Leave 'em dead with Levophed" and "Dread Phed." Nurses and doctors have sufficient experience with this drug to know most patients who receive it do not survive. They informed me Levo virtually clamps off the blood supply to the patient's hands and feet. A potential result might be the amputation of Bill's fingers or toes, if he survived (a **big** "if", I later learned). My response was, "What's my choice? Go ahead."

That evening, one of the nurses took my head in her hands and told me, "Bill may go to God tonight." Both my sister, Sue, and Skip stayed with me all night, alternately holding my hand and Bill's. I whispered in his ear if he needed to leave, I would try to understand, but I really wanted him to stay.

We went through twenty-four vials of a pressure-enhancing medication, at one point having it delivered by emergency courier from a nearby hospital. Sometime after midnight, Bill stabilized. When a suspicious-looking ART (arterial) line was removed the following morning, it turned out to be infected.

Within twenty-four hours of this first sepsis, his kidneys failed (acute kidney failure), his liver failed (shock liver), and his blood stopped clotting (Disseminated Intravascular Coagulation, or DIC). The doctors also suspected Bill had experienced a heart attack during sepsis as his body showed evidence of elevated levels of a heart enzyme that is present following myocardial episodes. Subsequently, I discovered he had suffered a stroke during this episode as well!

My research was producing statistics showing probable recovery for each of his organ failures and things had statistically moved well into the "probably will not survive this" realm. We were now in multi-organ failure syndrome—a very bad thing.

By this time, Bill was on a rotating bed to reduce the possibility of bedsores and improve his breathing. His color was that of the maroon fabric covering the bed. He received a dermatological consult to determine if the maroon skin color was a result of the sepsis or of a drug reaction. Although it was determined there was no drug reaction, he wore a wristband from that point forward warning of a possible allergy to a very powerful antibiotic.

The doctors soon started him on kidney dialysis that frequently dropped his blood pressure to a terrifyingly low level. They transfused him during dialysis to help his clotting factors, and we waited with crossed fingers to see if his liver function would return.

The following week brought his second sepsis, as critical as the first. This time, we did not have to go to the drug of last resort, Levophed. I found small comfort in that fact, when I learned he again had an infected ART line and, in all probability, had suffered another stroke. At that time, I thought it was the first stroke. Additionally, within twenty-four hours of this sepsis, Bill had two seizures while receiving dialysis. These seizures occurred when I was away from the hospital for the first time since his illness began. I'm surprised I wasn't killed in an automobile accident trying to get back to the hospital after receiving word of his condition.

I was terrified during the neurological consult following the seizure episodes, as the specialist explained all the possible causes and effects. Stroke damage, dead brain tissue, and brain damage all turned out not to be the case, but the possibilities were in play for several days while we awaited the test results. We never did know specifically what caused his seizures. In my research, I discovered any one of about ten of the conditions from which Bill was suffering could have been the cause. He was placed on anti-seizure medication for about a month after which it was d/c'd (discontinued) with no consequences.

The hospital Bill was in had two sleeping rooms with an adjoining bathroom made available to family members. I had moved into one of them following his second day there. I also shut down my consulting practice so I could be at the hospital full time.

During the rare uneventful moments at his bedside, I read about each catastrophe from material off the Internet. I also began asking questions of the doctors, identifying my sources of information as online articles and texts. I asked the nurses and technicians everything—how to read the monitors, what they meant, how to read his lab results, what they meant, how equipment in his room worked, what each line and drug was for, what each procedure was designed to demonstrate, and on and on and on. I had decided I wanted to know and understand as much as I could, since praying, and handholding seemed to be all I could otherwise do.

Bill got tons of visitors, a practice I had to stop since he was unconscious. We were both well beyond the point where visitors could comfort us. I always found myself recounting the most recent crises to these well-meaning people, resulting in more stress and anguish to me. Our primary care doctor had begun visiting us at the hospital, and I asked her for anti-depressant and anti-anxiety drugs. Frankly, at times my anti-anxiety medication was the only thing that kept me in my body.

The next weeks passed in a blur of tests, continuing sepsis, raging infections, fevers up to 105° Fahrenheit, anemia, pneumonia, and ileus (he stopped having bowel movements). The hospital also experienced a temporary, heart-stopping (mine, the respiratory therapist's, and Bill's nurse's) loss of electrical power during a circuit change where the maintenance crew forgot to inform the Intensive Care Unit to be on standby as equipment switched over to emergency power.

Fortunately, Bill's care providers were on the ball and came at a run, ready to manually bag him (manually push air into his lungs with a specially designed breathing bag) should the emergency power fail to kick on, putting the ventilator out of commission.

This experience taught me at a gut level the value of the electrical outlets with red-colored plates. These plates indicate electrical circuits that are connected to emergency power. Obviously, critical equipment such as a ventilator is plugged into red-plated outlets.

Bill's continued breathing difficulties prompted the pulmonologist (a doctor who specializes in the lungs) to perform a tracheostomy (an incision in the neck directly accessing the airway through which ventilator air is forced) so as to not ruin his voice box as a result of being orally ventilated (a breathing tube down the throat) for too long. When the doctors prepared Bill for the trach, they discovered he was "one in a million"—a vein ran right across the proposed trach site. This discovery delayed the trach procedure and caused terror regarding the possibility of a terminal hemorrhage, should the specialist performing the trach hit the vein. A thoracic surgeon (a specialist who conducts surgery on the chest) was called in on consult, and oversaw the procedure, which ultimately was performed without a hitch.

This was the first of many times where I was told, "Your husband's condition is one in a million." I came to associate those words with only the smallest chance for survival.

A common occurrence in extreme acute pancreatitis cases (of which Bill's was one) is the development of what is called pseudocysts, free-floating pieces of dead pancreatic tissue surrounded by liquid and blood in the abdominal area. During this time, it was suspected that Bill had developed one of these. It burst, causing another sepsis.

He ultimately developed four pseudocysts. Since the staff at the hospital was uncertain about the next course of treatment, they suggested when (if) Bill's condition improved, I move him to one of two hospitals where they had more experience treating his problem. One of these hospitals was local, one was out of state.

That day came on December 12, 2000, when I airlifted him via Lifeflight to an out-of-state hospital well known for taking only the most critically ill. I will never forget seeing him lying on the tarmac, strapped to a stretcher, attached to a ventilator, pale as death with eyes wide open in excitement at flying. Bill has always loved to fly, and even as sick and drugged as he was, he had some awareness of his surroundings. As we lifted off, I prayed I would be bringing Bill back from this consult alive, fearful he would return in a body bag.

Upon arrival at the new facility, Bill promptly went septic again. However, unlike at the previous hospital, I was initially not allowed in his Intensive Care room. That finally changed, but I will save that story for another chapter. Over the next ten ugly days, his diagnosis was totally rejected until the specialists at this facility could confirm it for themselves. In the meantime, Bill was poked, prodded, X-rayed, CT scanned, bled, and needle-aspirated (the withdrawal of liquid from his abdomen through a long needle, performed to determine the contents of the pseudocyst). The diagnosis was essentially, "There is nothing we can do for your husband. If you cut him open, he will die. Take him home and let him die peacefully."

During the course of Bill's stay at this hospital, he was denied critical treatment (dialysis) and medically necessary equipment (rotating bed), resulting in the need for cardioversion (electric clappers to the chest) when his heart rate exceeded 160 beats/minute for about an hour and the development of a first-stage (there are three stages, third being the worst) pressure wound (bedsore). All this occurred while I struggled to gain access to his room, his records, and his lab and test results— information I required to be an informed healthcare partner.

I airlifted Bill home with an immense sigh of relief. Upon returning home, we picked up the same three primary physicians who had previously worked with Bill but at a different hospital (my choice) so as to have more around-the-clock doctor coverage available, should we need it. Bill's condition continued to deteriorate (I always wondered if that was possible, given all he had already experienced) until January 12, 2001. On that day, I was informed his pseudocysts were no longer sterile (not infected) but had become infected. Surgery was no longer an option, but a necessity.

I was told, "If you do *not* cut him open, he will die." Reflecting on the previous hospital's diagnosis, "If you cut him open, he will die," from reported world-class experts, this was a certain-to-die situation. Recognizing I would most probably be moving him to his last living space, I had to choose between two locations for surgery: the place from which we had recently returned and a local teaching hospital.

For a long time, I had felt I had made a mistake transporting him to the prior hospital—a mistake until faced with this choice. I now believed the previous hospital would kill him and the only choice was our local option. The hospital arranged ambulance service, and I moved Bill once again. Bill was now sixty pounds lighter than on the day he was first admitted to the hospital. His waistline was so enlarged (ascites) it looked like he was fifteen months pregnant with triplets. He was still unconscious, still on full life support, still receiving daily kidney dialysis, and still receiving massive blood transfusions.

Bill was being fed with a feeding tube inserted in his abdomen, a procedure done the day prior to transfer, during which the doctor feared he had punctured Bill's colon.

Upon arrival at the fourth and final hospital, every department head consulted on Bill's case during the first three hours—a far cry from the reported world-famous out-of-state facility in which he had previously been hospitalized. The surgeon came to me and said, "Your husband is about as sick as anyone can be and still be alive." His assistants scurried around, securing my permission to operate and advising me of the less than 5 percent survival rate. At this point, we were so past probable survival I could barely digest the information. All I could do was get a room in the hospital, pray, and try to get rest for the next day, in all probability Bill's last day on this earth.

The following morning (Saturday—not a day ordinarily chosen for surgery, which shows how time-critical this procedure was deemed to be), Bill was alert, so we told him what we were going to do—cut out the growths in his abdomen that were causing all the problems. I kissed him (and prayed it wasn't goodbye).

Then I joined thirteen friends and family members who miraculously showed up to provide support—miraculous in that they had flown in from all over the country with less than twenty-four hours' notice, miraculous in that nurses from three hospitals back were present, miraculous in that they all loved both of us, even though the original friendships had begun with either one or the other of us. When the surgeon emerged following the surgery, his first response was, "Wow! What a crowd!"

We filled the waiting room, waiting to hear if the 5 percent survival rate had prevailed with my honey, my husband, my

Bill. When told Bill had done well throughout the surgery, a collective cry went up. The doctor described removing four basketball-sized pseudocysts from Bill's abdomen and packing it with surgical gauze to absorb the drainage and allow the swelling to go down. He stated he would have to go back into the surgical site in two days to remove the gauze and close the wound. He sat with all of us patiently, answering questions for twenty minutes. We hail this man as the person who saved Bill's life.

Even though Bill went septic that night and on many subsequent occasions, this surgery marked the turning point for his extraordinary recovery. Literally, from the moment he left surgery, Bill began to heal.

Several days after he finally awoke from the surgery, Bill began to write me notes. He was so weak his letters were only about an eighth of an inch high and they all ran together. The poor guy couldn't figure out why I couldn't read them! He was now strong enough to ask the nurse to turn his bed around so he could look out at the helipad and watch helicopters arrive with hospital patients.

He began physical and occupational therapy in earnest. I learned about and helped with his exercises and was the sole administrator of the same on weekends and holidays when the physical therapy (PT) and occupational therapy (OT) staff was not present.

I learned how to dress Bill's surgical sites and came to know the names and understand the purposes of eleven drainage tubes and pumps implanted in his abdomen. I learned how to "deep suction" his trach and empty the traps of the water collected in his ventilator tubing. By this time, he had developed MRSA (methicillin or multi-resistant staphylococcus aureus, called the "hospital acquired infection" or, in doctor's language, "nosocomial"), so I had to wear a gown, mask and gloves when in his room.

I had become quite handy at assisting with patient movement, foot massage, and boot replacement and removal (a device placed on the feet of long-term hospital patients designed to prevent blood clots).

My skills and Bill's condition improved daily, so much so that by early March—five months after his initial hospital admission—he was strong enough to transfer out of the hospital to the Rehabilitation Unit. Even his kidneys began working again and, although not perfect, they were functioning well enough to discontinue dialysis.

Always the optimist, I believed Bill's progress was now a certainty, although he still had occasional line infections and continual feeding tube problems. Slowly, doctors removed tubes and weaned him off the ventilator. He continued to improve. In late March, exhausted but comfortable with Bill's condition, I went to New Mexico for four days to relax (collapse was more like it).

On the Thursday following my trip, Bill complained to both me and the nurses of being quite tired. He was too tired to do his therapy both Thursday and Friday. Since this was not an uncommon complaint, neither the other healthcare providers nor I took it too seriously. On Friday, he complained of a headache and was quite crabby. Unusual for me, I chose to go home that night and sleep in our bed because his behavior had worn me out.

At 6:30 the next morning, the phone beside my bed rang. A nurse was telling me I had better get to the hospital as fast as I could, because Bill had coded in the Rehab Unit and been readmitted to the hospital Intensive Care Unit. I threw on clothes and flew to the hospital. Once I got there, the doctor treating Bill told me that on a routine middle-of-the-night check, the care partner had come in to take his temperature and check his pulse and found him barely breathing. She called a code, at which point he began having seizures and stopped breathing.

The doctors could barely get the ventilator tube down his throat (his trach had grown shut) because of his seizures, and his oxygen level registered at less than 60 percent. This could mean anywhere from 60 percent to one percent, since the equipment is not sufficiently sensitive to measure below the 60 percent level. Because the medical team responding to the code could not get Bill's seizures under control, they artificially induced a coma. No one could give me a cause or a prognosis, physical or mental.

Bill was kept comatose and ventilated for six days while the doctors searched for a medication that would control his seizure activity. For some reason, his previously injured liver just ate up seizure medication, as it does to this day.

It took four tries, but finally Bill was "loaded" with a therapeutic level of Dilantin, the drug he had taken for the seizures of the prior year. He was finally weaned off his sedatives and returned to consciousness.

The next few weeks were ghastly, for Bill and all the rest of us. Bill continually reported he was in Chicago (we were in Kansas City) and he wanted to go downtown and get some pizza (he was still NPO—nothing by mouth). He insisted on walking to the bathroom "like a man" (he couldn't even sit up unaided), and he saw and heard a skinny little man under my bed who blew on an empty pop bottle during the night.

This behavior was due to documented evidence that Bill had right temporal and right parietal lobe damage (parts of the brain) damage caused by suspected endocarditis (an infection in a heart valve, probably caused by one of his septic episodes), part of which had broken loose and seeded itself in multiple locations of his brain, causing an infection, seizures and another stroke. The doctors informed me it would be six to twelve months before we knew the true impact of this horrible episode, while we waited to see if his brain would utilize its capability to re-grow new pathways.

I never dreamed I would get his body back for him, only to lose his mind.

Bill was confused and periodically pulled out tubes. I approved soft gloves lacking thumbs for restraint (hospitals are *very* cautious about the use of restraints). He soon figured out how to get those off and would try to get out of bed without help. I had to approve a more aggressive method of restraint: Bill's hands and feet were tied to the bed. Fortunately and surprisingly, his kidneys continued working throughout this trauma. His speech, occupational, and physical therapists demonstrated great patience with his mentally limited repertoire. Slowly, slowly, Bill came around.

Due to his diligent progress, the hospital discharged Bill on June 6, 2001, exactly eight and a-half months after admission.

Sadly, Bill was readmitted to the hospital for a week in late June, then for a day in early October, both times following seizures at home. I learned how to administer IVs, give shots, and dress wounds at home. I also learned the response drill for seizures and hope I do not get any more experience using it.

Today, nearly four years later, Bill struggles with the reality of a changed life. The blessings are immense, and so are the losses. He had to wait for over a year and a-half to drive because he had to be seizure-free for six consecutive months before he was cleared to drive again. He recently had an accident in my car due to an "absence seizure" (he was unaware of his surroundings) caused by taking the generic equivalent of his seizure medication. Although no one was hurt (but my car to the tune of $12,000), he now has to wait another six months to drive. He has broken his feet three times due to the combination of not getting enough weight-bearing activity and the onset of osteoporosis from substandard feeding tube nutrition for six months (although higher levels of nutrition might have placed too much stress on his newly-recovered kidneys).

He receives private disability and Social Security, something we never thought we would see in our lifetimes. Since leaving the hospital, Bill has done extensive physical therapy and has taken up yoga. He still tires easily. He continues to grapple with balance issues. His depression and anger are overwhelming for both of us. However, there is a bottom line, and it is this:

- Never, never give up! There are miracles in the world, and Bill is one of them!

- You or your family member *can* experience a miracle! Always believe!

- Life is a gift! Seek it!

> "What I am trying to say is hard
> To tell and hard to understand...
> Unless, unless you have been
> Yourself at the edge of the deep
> Canyon and have come back
> Unharmed. Maybe it all depends
> On something within yourself –
> Whether you are trying to see
> the water snake or the sacred Cornflower,
> whether you go out
> to meet death or to seek life."
>
> —Author Unknown

CHAPTER 3
Take Care of Yourself

If you are not good for yourself, how can you be good for another?
—Spanish Proverb

Fear is that little darkroom where negatives are developed.
—Michael Pritchard

RECOMMENDATION #1: TAKE CARE OF YOURSELF. You are of no value to your loved one if you go down for the count. Sacrificing your own health for another is not what anyone who loves us would want us to do.

Take care of yourself is the first and last recommendation, because all other recommendations depend on it. This is **not**

a self-help book designed to assist you in discovering what gives you strength or refreshes you when your energy is low. I sincerely hope you already know these things. This book is about caring for another who needs your help. You cannot do that if you do not care for yourself first.

There were five areas in which I needed personal assistance, at various times more so than others.

1. **At home**
2. **At the hospital**
3. **Physically**
4. **Emotionally**
5. **Spiritually**

Regardless of which area was "up" at any particular time, one source of assistance was constantly available—my friends. I have historically been a very independent person, so much so that I insisted on being the one who offered the assistance. Accepting assistance was a foreign concept to me. As a consultant working with employees in the "soft side" of business, behavioral change, I always kept myself sane by saying, "People don't change unless the pain of remaining the same exceeds the pain of doing things differently." Well, the pain of remaining the same in each of these areas was

waaaayyy more painful than accepting a little help from my friends. Please let others "do" for you during this time.

1. At Home

I hope you will not be involved with your family member's illness as long as I was. However, if you stay at the hospital, find a neighbor or family member or friend who can collect your mail, bring in your paper and generally make your home look occupied while you are gone.

Our first "home" crisis occurred when I decided to stay at the hospital and had to get someone to take care of our dogs. Bill and I have four dogs. We consider them part of our family and call them our kids. Several people, including two of Bill's colleagues who greatly dislike dogs, offered to help. Ultimately, I was able to get in touch with our former dog sitter, April, who took care of our kids for eight months. I loaned April Bill's truck for that period of time, a trade that proved very acceptable for all parties.

Since April was going in and out of the house three times a day, she would turn lights on and off. Sometimes she would leave the truck in the driveway, sometimes in the garage, to create inconsistency should someone be watching the house. Additionally, I kept Lisa, the woman who cleans our house, on a regular cleaning schedule. This ensured nothing broke irrevocably (like the water pipes when we got an unexpected hard freeze and had not turned off the spigots to the outside faucets). Between them, April and Lisa ordered dog food, maintained the premises and the canines, and prevented a burglary by noticing signs and taking appropriate actions.

One of the pride and joys in life is my greenhouse. Bill built it for me and customized it to meet my every desire. I have hundreds of plants, all requiring regular attention. I am grateful my friend Kevin came to our house weekly and watered my plants. In addition, April had instructions to turn the greenhouse lights on and off and activate the heater, when necessary. This was another thing that made the house appear occupied.

When spring came and I could spare a little time away from the hospital readying the house for Bill's homecoming, my sister's family and our friends spent many hours planting our annual garden, cleaning the gutters, and raking the leaves from the previous fall—all things that had gone undone during Bill's hospitalization.

2. At the Hospital

When you are living at the hospital, you still need to eat and wear clean clothes. Eating at our first, under populated hospital was a problem because the cafeteria only served breakfast and lunch—and only on weekdays. Friends brought me food galore, and my sister did my laundry. She also picked up medications I needed from our pharmacy. Life would have been difficult without everyone's help.

Also, consider your physical comfort in the hospital room. Hospital #4 had what they called Chair Beds. These were chairs that converted into beds by pulling out a section and rearranging the cushions. Even if you do not plan to sleep at the hospital, I found it a real benefit to have one of these Chair Beds in Bill's room for an occasional catnap.

Security is an issue, outside when arriving or leaving the hospital at night as well as within the patient's room. Stay alert when entering or exiting the hospital, especially at night. Ask a security guard to accompany you to your car—you are particularly vulnerable if you are preoccupied, grieving, or in any way inattentive. Carry your personal items (such as your purse and computer) with you at all times. Patient room thefts were reported to me in two hospitals.

Additionally, carry anything with a credit card number on it out of the hospital and take it home to shred. I had a credit card number lifted from a torn receipt that had been placed in a contaminated bag. This means the thief had to expose him or herself to infection, blood, feces, and pus on the off chance something of value might be in the bag! The thief used it to purchase a $3,000 computer online. Fortunately, I caught the fraudulent charge early and my credit card company removed it from my bill.

3. Physically

As the stress of Bill's condition began to take its toll on me, I became a physical basket case. I couldn't wear my contacts because the hospital air was too dry. Friends brought me hand lotion and lip balm for the same complaint. My neck, previously injured in an auto accident, was so tight that there were days when I couldn't turn my head. I asked friends for a referral to a massage therapist but then I would not leave the hospital. With a couple of calls, I found a massage therapist who brought her table to the hospital, set it up, and gave me a massage in the room where I slept. Technically, she should not have done this, as she was not an employee of the hospital. However, she recognized my situation and took a risk.

Do what you can to dissipate the stress. We all carry stress in a different part of our body. It is usually carried in a location where a previous injury exists. If the hospital has a fitness center, ask if you can have a temporary membership. Take care of your body lest you become a patient yourself.

Wash your hands! This will help protect you and your loved one from catching anything. Hospital-acquired infections, such as MRSA, are transmitted by failure to maintain a sterile environment. If you have someone living at home who has a compromised immune system, I recommend removing and sanitizing your shoes following a hospital visit. Also, change out of and launder any clothing that may have touched the patient such as a tie.

Drink lots of water. Hospitals are notoriously dry, and lack of water can take an incredible toll when coupled with stress. Give your body the water it needs. Find the water cooler on each floor and use it. I never realized how little water I drank until every ounce/milliliter of liquid was measured as intake for my husband.

Find something to do in the hospital room. I did everything I could to help and even then I had huge amounts of time left over. Find the hospital library, which will contain magazines and books available for checkout to family members. Walk the hospital and you will find magazines in every waiting room. I borrowed these magazines freely and, as long as I returned them, there was never a complaint. Additionally, I added to the magazine stash in the waiting rooms from my own subscription collection. Make sure you remove your name and address from both the mailing label and the order form before donating to the cause.

Ground yourself. There is a well-known syndrome in Intensive Care units called "Sundowner's Syndrome." "Sundowning" is a state of increased agitation, activity and negative behaviors that happen late in the day through the evening hours. It used to be thought that sundowning was caused by the lowering light and shorter days. However, research now indicates that being overly tired may have more to do with sundowning.

Bill suffered from this on several occasions and still does, to some extent, at home when he gets overly tired. Guess who else was susceptible to Sundowner's? I was, and you will be, too, if you allow your 24/7 duty to keep you from leaving your loved one's room. At least once a day, step outside, pause, take a walk, and orient yourself to the world outside your microcosm. It helps with perspective and it helps to ground yourself.

One last thing about grounding yourself. Know what stress does to you and how the outside world responds to your reactions.

I know this sounds weird, but in addition to my bad neck, I tend to have an unexplained "hot" electrical charge when I am anxious. I have clients who do not allow me around electronic equipment as I tend to "blow" electrical devices. I cannot replace light bulbs at home as they always blow. I frequently blow overhead projector bulbs, copy machines, and street lamps.

No matter where I stayed during Bill's illness, there were electrical problems. I was terrified about this, as it affected devices in Bill's hospital room, devices that were keeping him alive. Going outside and grounding myself, therefore, was not only critical to my health, but to Bill's survival. In addition to visualizing myself connecting to the ground, a friend taught me to take three deep breaths. Upon exhalation, I visualized pushing all my stress into the ground. I can't tell you how much this simple exercise helped.

4. Emotionally

I am not a trained medical professional. Although I was certified as an Emergency Medical Technician at one point in my career twenty years ago, I never used this knowledge and remember very little. Even if I had been trained, my husband's case was so complex I needed a trusted medical adviser to help me think through problems and select the right solutions.

For me, that was our family physician and a friend who is a nurse practitioner. I discussed every incident with these two special and patient partners. My family physician also scripted, without office visits, the "little orange pills" (anti-anxiety) that prevented me from leaving my overly anxious body.

Without the help of these two trusted medically trained professionals, I would not have felt as confident about the decisions I made regarding Bill's healthcare and would have second-guessed myself, especially had Bill died.

I am not implying the specialists treating Bill were not extremely competent and helpful. They kept him viable through catastrophic medical events! However, they were very clear about the limit of their ability to provide medical care and they provided excellent options. However, options in the plural required decisions in the singular—decisions only I could make. Without my medical partners/friends, I would have been lost.

We can only run on our emotional reserves for so long. It was terrifying and nerve-racking not to know what caused Bill's illness. When the doctors thought this would take "the normal run for pancreatitis" which amounts to seven to ten days in the hospital, there were lots of folks around to help, but I didn't open myself up to them.

When the catastrophes commenced and continued, I went to my emotional well so many times, it dried up collapsed into itself. That was when I had to learn to accept emotional support, a hard lesson for me. As a self-employed, stubbornly independent female who had fought for everything I ever got, leaning on others was a foreign concept.

The first "lean" occurred during Bill's first two septic events. Both my sister and Skip were by my side that night, literally telling me what to do, as I was too numb and terrified to do for myself. "Jari, why don't you go and take a tranquilizer? You don't have to take a whole one (they tended to knock me out), just enough to take the edge off," which is what I did and how I survived.

After that, not only did I accept a strong shoulder, I even occasionally sought one to lean on. When I flew Bill to the out-of-state hospital, I racked up $500 in cell phone charges, calling people just to talk, to lean on. By the time Bill went in for his surgery, thirteen people came on behalf of Bill and to support me. This was a tremendous help, for had the outcome been different, I would have needed to lean on more than one person.

On and on throughout Bill's illness, unsolicited kindness and compassion came my way. This was good, since I hardly knew how to ask for it. Even had I not been so needy, the sheer volume of love eventually would have gotten through. How nice it would have been if I had been able to accept it from the beginning. The Pueblo Indians speak the truth when they say, *"The step beyond surrender is often magic."*

5. Spiritually

The seriousness of a life-threatening illness will test and confirm your spiritual belief, even if you have to pull it out and dust it off from years of disuse.

Regardless of the nature of your spiritual belief, finding the chapel in the hospital should be one of the first things you do. Whether you define "God" according to Christianity, Judaism, or spiritualism, whether you have any kind of faith in a Higher Power greater than yourself or simply need some peace and quiet, the chapel offers solace at whatever level you desire.

In not one of the four hospitals did a chaplain ever enter the chapel while I sat in there. For me, that was a relief as I went to the chapel for solitude. Just sitting quietly helped me with perspective and gave me relief from the noise of the machines keeping my husband alive. The chaplain did visit Bill's hospital room in each hospital, asking whether spiritual support was desired. That is the best time to work out the level of support you and your loved one desire.

The question, "Why me?" was especially troublesome when communing with my Higher Power one particular day. I was reminded of a lesson I learned shortly after I began my business in 1986. I was approached by a company to help set up the human resource function, and served as a consultant for six months.

As part of this project, I created the company's first-ever employee handbook, which contained, among other things, an AIDS (Acquired Immune Deficiency Syndrome, also known as HIV in the early stages) policy. At that time, the country was viewing AIDS differently than other terminal or disabling diseases. Thus the need for a separate policy.

There were some difficulties with this assignment so, as I did with all completed assignments, I turned around and looked back at it, conducting what I call an "Autopsy of Events." Since I have this theory that if I get it right, I may not have to repeat painful events, I do this following each assignment, so I can see what I learned or what I was supposed to learn. Try as I may, I could not find any significant learning for myself on this assignment. Troubled but not overly so, I moved on to my next assignment and gave it no more thought.

About two and a-half months after my departure from that client, one of the officers asked me to call another of the officers from the company at an unfamiliar phone number. I called, and the officer informed me he was in the hospital and wanted me to visit. The evening I visited him, he disclosed he had contracted AIDS and was in the final stage of the disease, with little time left.

We cried together, and he hugged me when I left, thanking me for implementing the AIDS policy so he could die in peace, knowing he and his family would not suffer financially in his final days. I left the hospital, shaken to the core. Not only was this the first "real" person I had known who contracted AIDS, this was someone who attributed his peaceful departure to me.

For many days, I grappled with the sorrow of his pending death, and then I realized he had given me an enormous gift. For what I was supposed to learn in that assignment was that everything in this life is *not about me!* In this case, I was just the servant who did my job. In doing so, I stumbled upon the right thing to do, convinced the company it was so, and set in motion a chain of events that neither I nor the employer ever expected to have to face.

I tell this story as a way of illustrating that the hospitalization of your loved one *may not be about you!* You may be an innocent bystander. But remember, bystanders save strangers' lives every day, and your family member is hardly a stranger. Do what you can. In the process, you, too, may receive an enormous gift, the gift of life.

Spirituality also came to me and at me through the other people who were trying to cope with the critical nature of Bill's illness. Each of us will seek spirit in our own way and who's to say which way is the right one?

I honor all the prayers said for Bill and I, whether spoken in English or not, whether said in a church or a synagogue or in bed at night, whether spoken by a Muslim or a Catholic. My "God" heard and answered them all.

Checklist A that follows reflects the five areas in which I needed personal assistance.

CHECKLIST A—Taking Care of Me

CATEGORY	ARRANGEMENTS NEEDED	√
AT HOME	Children	
AT HOME	Elderly	
AT HOME	Pets	
AT HOME	Plants	
AT HOME	Lights	
AT HOME	Mail	
AT HOME	House maintenance	
AT HOME		
AT HOME		
AT HOME		
AT THE HOSPITAL	Food	
AT THE HOSPITAL	Sleeping arrangements	
AT THE HOSPITAL	Round-the-clock patient coverage	
AT THE HOSPITAL	Personal belongings–purse, computer	
AT THE HOSPITAL	Journal, paper, pen, and tape for signs	
AT THE HOSPITAL		
AT THE HOSPITAL		
PHYSICALLY	Reading materials	
PHYSICALLY	Stress relief	
PHYSICALLY	Grounding	
PHYSICALLY	Wash hands frequently	

Take Care of Yourself

CATEGORY	ARRANGEMENTS NEEDED	√
PHYSICALLY	Drink adequate water	
PHYSICALLY	Medications	
PHYSICALLY	Walking outside	
PHYSICALLY		
PHYSICALLY		
PHYSICALLY		
EMOTIONALLY	Family phone numbers	
EMOTIONALLY	Friends' phone numbers	
EMOTIONALLY	Trusted medical advisor[s] phone number	
EMOTIONALLY		
EMOTIONALLY		
EMOTIONALLY		
SPIRITUALLY	Location of chapel	
SPIRITUALLY	Spiritual advisor[s] phone number	
SPIRITUALLY	Notification of church	
SPIRITUALLY		
SPIRITUALLY		
SPIRITUALLY		

CHAPTER 4
Choose Your Hospital with Awareness

He who asks a question is a fool for five minutes;
he who does not ask a question remains a fool forever.

—Chinese Proverb

RECOMMENDATION #2: CHOOSE YOUR HOSPITAL WITH AWARENESS. Under populated hospitals offer far more care, at the expense of far less doctor presence. Over populated hospitals offer far more doctor presence, at the expense of care. I've never found an appropriately populated hospital. Which is more important for your loved one–care or doctor's presence?

The meaning of the above statement may seem obscure at first. After all, aren't all hospitals the same? I am a highly educated and experienced business professional who knows, without the shadow of a doubt, that each business is different. However, I had never considered the same as it relates to hospitals.

During the course of Bill's hospitalization, we were in four different hospitals. Two were intentional, two accidental. During that time, I learned a great deal about the differences between hospitals. Each hospital has strengths and weaknesses and not all hospitals are available to you as an "in-plan" hospital through your insurance carrier.

When you have a choice of hospitals, do your homework. Prior to hospitalization, make decisions with your loved one about what matters most to them about their support and recovery. Just because the physician you prefer practices at a certain hospital does not ensure that the hospital is a viable choice for you. It may simply be a hospital in which the doctor has a financial interest. Given time, there are always options. Know as much as you can about what the patient will need, and emphasize it in your hospital choice. Otherwise, you may get great nurses and few doctors when it is the choice of a doctor that will increase the odds for recovery.

The one absolute requirement for the hospital of choice should be accreditation with the Joint Commission on Accreditation of Healthcare Organizations (JCAHO). This group inspects and certifies healthcare facilities against predetermined standards.

Contact the JCAHO at their general information number (630-792-5000) or via their web site (http://www.jcaho.org) to review the most up-to-date accreditation results.

The balance of this chapter identifies the strengths and weaknesses of each of the four hospitals in which Bill was treated, as seen through my eyes. It is critical to review the defining characteristics of the hospital you and your loved one select, in order to make the choice most likely to result in recovery and a return to health. The following comparisons identify what I believed to be most important to Bill and me. These comparisons should assist you in identifying the defining characteristics of the hospital you require.

HOSPITAL #1, Private Facility

Hospital #1 was the hospital located closest to Bill's workplace. We did not choose it—he was transported there in an emergency mode. It was at this hospital Bill first received treatment from what I came to call his primary doctors: a gastrointestinal (GI or "gut") specialist, a nephrologist (kidney specialist), and a pulmonologist (respiratory or lung specialist).

STRENGTHS	WEAKNESSES
New facility.	During the day, the only doctor available in the hospital was the one making rounds at the time.
Very low patient count.	On nights, weekends, and holidays, only one doctor in the hospital, who leaves the Emergency Room only when a patient codes.
Lower nurse-to-patient ratio; lots of attention given to patients.	Cost of services/equipment comparatively very high.
Sleeping rooms available at no charge for family members.	The primary doctor's partners in several cases were substantially substandard compared to the attending specialist; you were stuck with them if you wanted to keep the primary specialist.
State-of-the-art equipment.	Few supplies, often had to make do, or order from sister facility.
Fewer "resident" germs (the older a facility, the higher the probability germs survive in rooms long after the departure of the patient who introduced them).	When medical crises occurred, medical personnel contacted doctors at home. Doctors either offered advice from home or had to drive back to the hospital, slowing down treatment response time.
Spacious patient rooms, even in ICU.	No one had vast amounts of experience treating Bill's specific disease.

Choose Your Hospital with Awareness

STRENGTHS	WEAKNESSES
Loose patient visitation practices; 24 hour access.	Had to shut off visitation by the many friends that asked questions and wore me out.
Outstanding skilled nursing care.	Frequently ran out of linens.
Support network available.	Limited cafeteria menu and hours.
Reasonable consistency in the time at which doctors made rounds.	Vigilance by chaplain although caring was stifling. For others, this level of attention may be comforting.
Continuity/consistency of nursing care (the same nurses were assigned to Bill virtually every day so we did not have to continuously bring new players up to speed).	Loose protocol around contagion. Bill developed the hospital infection MRSA while here; family was not informed of proper protocol nor was it enforced.
Primary doctors frequently made rounds together and, thus, consulted each other frequently on Bill's condition.	If I was tired or upset and didn't want to talk about Bill's condition, I couldn't avoid it for all the questions by caring staff.
Easy access to management and administration.	Substandard medical library for research.

24/7 or Dead

STRENGTHS	WEAKNESSES
Friendliness (everyone in the hospital knew and asked about Bill daily).	Family was aware of professional and personal differences between staff members.
Willingness to allow me immediate access to medical resource material.	Access did not always result in what I believed to be appropriate actions.
Use of and tolerance for digital cell phones (that do not interfere with medical equipment).	
Presence of "hospitalists", general practitioners who oversee all specialists and treatment for a given case	
Pharmacy and laboratory staffs responded quickly to requests.	
Taught me about equipment and treatments, encouraged and allowed me to help with care.	
Allowed me to remain in Bill's room during procedures.	

OSPITAL #2, World-renowned teaching/research facility

Hospital #2 was the hospital to which Bill was airlifted and was recommended as a facility with extensive experience in treating Bill's illness. I chose this facility over Hospital #4 based on reputation.

Choose Your Hospital with Awareness

STRENGTHS	WEAKNESSES
Presence of many specialists with extensive experience treating Bill's disease.	Very old facility.
Round-the-clock, high quality doctor availability.	Consistently high patient count.
Presence of pulmonologists (respiratory specialists), who ran the Intensive Care Unit	Shocking and derogatory denigration of family involvement.
Tight protocol around contagion, consistently enforced.	Higher patient-to-nurse ratio; not as much attention given to patients.
Facilities, equipment, and supplies available at all hours.	Refusal to provide preventive care (Bill was not allowed to have a rotating bed) due to rigid and unbending rules around what constitutes need (Bill's bedsores began here); Bill was denied timely kidney dialysis.
Adequate patient room size in ICU.	Bill was a number, not a person; very impersonal.
Extensive experience treating shock, sepsis, and other frequent maladies of critically ill patients.	Many young ICU nurses who lacked in-depth experience and were at this facility to get it.
Outstanding medical library for research.	Outright refusal to allow me access to Bill's medical records.
Decent but very expensive cafeteria menu; hours of operation corresponded to typical meal times.	Refusal to allow me access to Bill's ICU room overnight.

STRENGTHS	WEAKNESSES
Chaplain service available but not intrusive.	Required to sleep off campus, as no rooms were available for families in the hospital.
	No continuity of nursing care, even following request.
	Specialty doctors could not do anything without a consultation and approval from the pulmonologist in charge.
	Lots of "resident" germs.
	Restricted me from helping with Bill's care.
	Had to repeat information over and over, as multiple doctors from the same department at different levels of education made their rounds.
	Zero tolerance or allowance for digital cell phones (that do not interfere with medical equipment).
	Far from home and without our support network.

HOSPITAL #3, Private Facility

Hospital #3 was the hospital to which Bill was returned after the airlift. I chose this facility in consult with Bill's nephrologist after specifying both the need for more onsite doctor availability than Hospital #1 and a facility where that particular nephrologist practiced. By selecting this facility, Bill was again treated by his original team of three primary doctors.

STRENGTHS	WEAKNESSES
Many seasoned nurses.	Very old facility.
Round-the-clock, high quality doctor availability,	Grossly inadequate patient room size in ICU.
Tight protocol around contagion, consistently enforced.	Refusal to provide preventive care due to misinformation regarding ability of present bed to support healing of bedsores (Bill was not allowed to have a rotating bed and, as a result, his bedsores deteriorated here).
Adequate medical library for research.	No sleeping rooms available for family members; family encouraged to "go home."
Decent cafeteria menu; hours of operation corresponded to typical meal times, except on weekends and holidays.	Rigid patient visitation practices; banned from room during shift change, no matter the situation.

STRENGTHS	WEAKNESSES
Primary doctors treated me as a full partner regarding Bill's care.	Poor access to management and administration; fear of lawsuit overrode appropriate response regarding intrusive, offsite family members.
Support network available.	Inconsistency in the times at which doctors made rounds.
	Zero tolerance or allowance for digital cell phones (that do not interfere with medical equipment).
	Consistently banned from room during procedures, allegedly because of room size.
	The primary doctor's partners in several cases were substantially substandard compared to the attending specialist; you were stuck with them if you wanted to keep the primary specialist.
	No one had vast amounts of experience in treating Bill's disease.
	Never saw the hospital chaplain.
	Willingness to tolerate family involvement depended on nurse.
	No continuity of nursing care, even following request.

STRENGTHS	WEAKNESSES
	Refusal to allow me access to Bill's ICU room overnight.

HOSPITAL #4, University Facility

Hospital #4 was the hospital I chose when Bill's pancreatic pseudocysts became infected and surgery was mandatory. I was given the choice of Hospital #2 or Hospital #4. Since we had already been there and done that—miserably—with Hospital #2, there really was no choice. We were here for the longest period of time. Please note that we experienced all levels of care in Hospital #4, whereas Hospitals #1, #2, and #3 were only assessed according to treatment Bill received in Intensive Care.

STRENGTHS	WEAKNESSES
Immediate, head-of-department attention upon transfer; surgery performed on Saturday (*highly* unusual that any but the most critical services are performed on a weekend).	Very high patient count. Had to wait five days in the hospital, hoping for a discharge in the Rehabilitation Unit, in order to be admitted into the Rehabilitation Unit.

STRENGTHS	WEAKNESSES
Presence of many specialists with extensive experience in treating Bill's disease.	Had to repeat information over and over, as multiple doctors from the same department at different levels of education made their rounds.
Extensive experience treating shock, sepsis, and other frequent maladies of critically ill patients.	Frequently ran out of linens.
Many seasoned nurses.	Very old facility.
Round-the-clock, high quality doctor availability.	Doctors for each specialty, but no doctor assigned to oversee total treatment plan, except in ICU.
Tight protocol around contagion, consistently enforced.	Care partners (aides) were only intermittently helpful.
Decent cafeteria menu; hours of operation corresponded to typical meal times, except on weekends and holidays.	Boring menu, very repetitive.
Aggressive preventive care (Bill was immediately placed on a rotating bed which began the long-term healing process for his bedsores); specialty nurse made frequent visits.	In-charge doctors for each specialty rotated monthly; continuity of doctor care was inconsistent.
Flexible patient visitation practices outside ICU; allowed to sleep in Bill's room.	Rigid patient visitation practices in ICU; banned from room during shift change, no matter the situation.

STRENGTHS	WEAKNESSES
Sleeping rooms available to family members for a fee.	Limited number of rooms, often insufficient number.
Experimental treatment tried (with full consent) around topical (through the skin) bedsore treatment and topical delivery of medications while Bill was NPO (nothing by mouth).	Nursing was always short staffed and overworked. (This was more noticeable here because Bill was not in ICU for the entire time.)
Appropriate access to management and administration; insistence on patients' rights overrode the fear of lawsuit regarding intrusive, offsite family members.	Some nurses rejected family involvement in treatment; one nurse made unsubstantiated charge against family member involved in treatment.
Majority of nurses welcomed family involvement in treatment.	Occasionally, the need for speed overrode patient concerns; Bill was dropped and a tube was pulled out during a transfer.
Every attempt was made to provide continuity of nursing care following request.	Had to insist on the removal of one doctor and several nurses from providing care to Bill.
Officially, zero tolerance or allowance for digital cell phones (that do not interfere with medical equipment).	Unofficially, digital cell phones were tolerated outside ICU.

STRENGTHS	WEAKNESSES
Frequently asked about Bill's condition; frequently offered help while moving through hospital with Bill in wheelchair; we were known and cared for by name.	Aggressive and inappropriate bill collection protocol (e.g., "I will make a note on your file but I cannot prevent our computer from sending you a collection notice").
Support network available, both within and outside hospital; one nurse care coordinator followed us for six months.	Lots of "resident" germs.
Chaplain service available but not intrusive.	Periodically, Bill was the "lesson of the day" for medical students.

Now, what do you do with all of this? Based on these comparisons, create your own list of priorities for the hospital of your choice. Start by answering the following two questions:

1. What is most important to the recovery of your loved one, your number one choice of doctor or skilled nursing care?

2. How far is the recommended hospital from your home? Is it so far you will need help to manage the home front? (If so, see **Checklist A** at the end of Chapter 3.)

Next, using the comparisons I detailed in the tables found on the prior pages, list your hospital priorities on the following page, using **Checklist B**. At this point, all you are doing is specifying requirements for your own particular situation.

CHECKLIST B—Your Hospital Checklist

REQUIREMENT	STRENGTH √	WEAKNESS √	COMMENTS

How can you know how a hospital will treat you or your loved one until you actually experience it? To be very frank, you cannot. However, by asking questions of the doctor and the hospital, you can gain information so you are not operating totally in the dark (see **Checklists C** and **D**).

Why are we doing this? There is a legal tenet called "due diligence." It states that we have a responsibility for doing our homework. If we do not exercise this responsibility, we cannot complain about the outcome. It's kind of like the statement, "I vote so I can complain about the candidate's actions later." In this context, I am suggesting that you exercise due diligence. Your reward will be a facility where the best forces exist to support both the recovery of your family member and the efforts you will make on his or her behalf.

Let's start with the doctor who, in many cases, will recommend the hospital based upon where he/she has privileges (is authorized to practice medicine).

CHECKLIST C—Gathering Information About Your Doctor

QUESTIONS FOR THE DOCTOR	√ AND COMMENTS
With which hospital are you affiliated? Why?	
If multiple hospitals were available, which would you choose under these circumstances?	
Which circumstances are driving your recommendation?	
What are the drawbacks of the recommended hospital?	
Tell me about the other doctors with whom you must consult or work in order to provide treatment.	
How many cases like this have you treated in the last year?	
What kind of follow-up contact can we expect from you?	
What contact, if any, will we have with your partners?	
If appropriate, will I be allowed in the room during the procedure?	
Tell me about the quality of nursing care at the recommended hospital.	
Do you have a financial interest in this institution?	

The next checklist is for the hospital. But, whom do you ask? Do *not* go to Admission, Administration, or Public Relations.

Admission can only discuss the business aspects of the patient's stay. The goal of Administration and Public Relations is to promote the facility and, therefore, always put the best spin on things. You need honest answers. If your recommended hospital has care coordinators (nurses who coordinate care), ask to speak with the care coordinator assigned to the service (department) where your loved one is most likely to require the greatest care. Also, consider just hanging out in the hospital cafeteria or visiting a floor and paying attention. It is amazing what you can learn!

At Hospital #4, care coordinators (nurse specialists) were assigned to each of the specialties. I found them to be honest, straight shooters. If no care coordinators or "hospitalists" (general practice doctors who coordinate care) exist, seek information from the patient advocate providers since, after all, you may ultimately need their assistance.

Do not be afraid to bring your checklist with you. Introduce yourself, explain the purpose of your visit, and move into your questions. Remember, the people with whom you are meeting are employees of the hospital and expected to support it. Listen carefully to what they do *not* say.

Also, contact the Risk Management Department and ask about their infection control procedures.

24/7 or Dead

Be advised this is *very unusual* behavior for a family member, so you may meet with some resistance. Any sign of resistance is a potential indication of the hospital's unwillingness to partner with you. That, for me, is a big red flag!

CHECKLIST D—Gathering Information About Your Hospital

QUESTIONS FOR THE HOSPITAL	√ COMMENTS
Are you accredited by the Joint Commission on Accreditation of Healthcare Organizations (JCAHO)? When was your last inspection? (Also check with JCAHO)	
What are your visitation policies?	
Will I be allowed to assist with the care of my family member?	
What kind of continuity of nursing care can I expect?	
What kind of spiritual support does this facility provide?	
Tell me about the number of doctors and nurses present in the hospital on nights, weekends, and holidays. Can I expect treatment comparable to that during day shifts?	
May I look at a typical patient room?	
How old is this facility? When did you last remodel?	

Choose Your Hospital with Awareness

QUESTIONS FOR THE HOSPITAL	√ COMMENTS
What is the *registered* nurse-to-patient ratio in the specific service where my family member will be housed? (Be sure to specify RNs, as the nursing staff includes other personnel.)	
Tell me about (show me) your library.	
Tell me about your cafeteria. (Go eat there and check it out for yourself.)	
Will I be allowed to see the labs and test results myself?	
May I use my digital cell phone on the premises?	
Describe your infection control procedures.	
If I plan on sleeping at the hospital, do you have chair beds or rollaway beds or must I provide my own?	
Who will be the "general contractor" of my family member's healthcare (like the hospitalist or care coordinator)?	
What is the protocol if I am dissatisfied with the care my family member is receiving?	
Does your hospital have a computerized prescription system?	

Finally, return to **Checklist B** and satisfy yourself about each of your specified requirements—are they strengths or weaknesses? Place a check in the appropriate column and add any notes that will be helpful in your analysis.

CHAPTER 5
Pick the Days of Your Stay Carefully

A bad thing usually costs a lot.

—Unknown

RECOMMENDATION #3: PICK THE DAYS OF YOUR STAY CAREFULLY. Nothing happens in hospitals on nights, weekends, and holidays. Often, that includes the conduct of important procedures. Even hospitals with an appropriate doctor presence will be substandard on nights, weekends, and holidays. Particularly on holidays, the least experienced staff often provide care because those with seniority (experience) bid for the time off. Try for Monday admission.

Let me start out by saying *nothing* happens on nights, weekends, and holidays. When I say *nothing*, I mean *nothing*! In all our time in the hospital, only one thing happened on a weekend, and that was Bill's surgery. Frankly, had he not been so critically ill, I don't believe surgery would have happened on Saturday. In this case, Monday surgery would have cost Bill his life.

Because *nothing* happens on nights, weekends, and holidays, it is obviously in the patient's best interests not to be admitted immediately prior to any of these days (unless it is an emergency), and it is preferable to be discharged before any of these days. Nights, weekends, and holidays represent the time of lowest staffing and highest pay. Therefore, hospitals are routinely understaffed during these times, and patients are at their most vulnerable.

On Mother's Day in Hospital #4, there was one nurse on the entire floor of sixteen patients for twelve hours with one care partner. When do you suppose she got a break? How clear-headed, even with the best intentions, was she while distributing medications at 6 PM after ten hours alone?

This was especially true when one of her patients coded during the shift, requiring her to stay by his side and assist the emergency team for two hours until the patient was transferred to the ICU.

Pick the Days of Your Stay Carefully

I wonder who was attending to the other fifteen patients during this time? What would have happened if another patient had needed immediate care?

While Bill was in Hospital #1, we passed many holidays. During the night shift on Thanksgiving Day, one of the lines connected to Bill's triple lumen (a port that enables three lines to be connected out of one IV site) accidentally got caught in the mattress while it was rotating and was pulled out.

This was no one's fault. However, it represented an immediate need, as he was receiving both food and medications through this line. The ICU nurse first noticed it when she came to check on Bill and saw the line was leaking all over the bed. This particular ICU nurse was an agency nurse, meaning she subcontracted to the hospital through a nursing agency and was not an employee of the hospital. She was, however, very competent and had gained my respect by nursing Bill through the near-death experience of his second septic episode.

Being an agency nurse, she was required to notify the nurse manager in charge before she made any requests. The nurse manager came to Bill's room, verified the line was out and stated she would contact the hospitalist. I asked why she was contacting the hospitalist, since the three prior times the triple lumen was inserted, it was done by Anesthesia. She commented that the hospital was short staffed due to the holiday and proceeded to contact the hospitalist.

When she reached the hospitalist, I was not surprised that he recommended the triple lumen be replaced by Anesthesia. To her credit, the nurse manager did contact Anesthesia, who asked if the hospitalist could do the replacement. Clearly, she was getting the runaround.

At that point, the nurse manager made a decision with which I disagreed. Instead of insisting that Anesthesia come and replace the line, she disconnected the call with Anesthesia and stated, "It's a holiday and people are at home with their families, where they should be." When I asked if she was suggesting Bill could not get a medically necessary treatment because it was a holiday, she reiterated they were short staffed because of the holiday and the triple lumen replacement could wait until the following morning.

By now, as a result of the missing IV line, Bill's blood pressure was up as he had been denied bicarbonate to moderate the acid in his body; he had been without IV-administered food for over two hours; and he was about to miss his antibiotic treatment. As a tired, anxious and frightened spouse, I lost it and replied, "No, it can't!" I went on to ask if this was indeed a 24-hour Intensive Care Unit and demanded she get help.

I had previously witnessed this nurse manager try to pull nurses off of Bill's care during emergencies, stating, "It only takes one person to care for him"—this during a septic episode where there were five nurses and a doctor in the room, barely keeping up with the required treatments. She had also admonished me for washing my hands in the utility room when the sink in Bill's room was unavailable and being used for dialysis. Additionally, she had lectured me on my responsibility to change the sheets in the room where I was sleeping, instead of "bothering the housekeeping staff who had enough work tending the real patients' rooms."

At my insistence, the nurse manager again called the hospitalist. While we waited for his return call, the agency nurse started an IV line. When she stated we needed another line in addition to the one she had just started, I said, "No." If the triple lumen was replaced, we would be able to stop "sticking" Bill (hospital slang for inserting a needle), a patient who, for many reasons by now, was a very hard "stick" (meaning it was hard to find a suitable blood vessel).

Rather than contacting the pharmacy staff of her own hospital who were not present at that time but available by pager—remember, it was a holiday—the nurse manager called the pharmacies in two other sister hospitals to see if there was an alternative method of delivery for the antibiotic. This question was asked within my earshot, without informing them of the full situation. Neither pharmacy was aware of any other delivery method.

An hour and a-half went by. When the anesthesiologist and hospitalist arrived, the triple lumen was replaced. When the hospitalist asked the nurse manager why Bill's primary doctor had not been called, her response was, "I'm not waiting around here anymore. I'm going home to be with my family. Here's my home phone number. He (Bill's primary doctor) can call me at home if he wants."

This episode brought me to the hospital administrator's office the next day where, following my report of the episode, I requested that the nurse manager not be allowed to treat or consult in any way on Bill's case. This request was honored for the duration of his stay and I was subsequently informed that the nurse manager had been suspended for her actions concerning this incident and was eventually terminated.

Although not typical, this incident represents the potential for problems during holiday shifts. The same holds true for nights and weekends. I ended up calling Hospital #4's pharmacy manager at home one Saturday midnight when, for the fourth time, the nurse was informed that one of Bill's medications was not available until Monday. The nursing staff listened to my complaint, raised their hands in support during the phone conversation with the pharmacy manager and subsequently reported to me that "this happens all the time" but, since they were hospital employees, they were afraid to report it!

If the hospital staff is discussing the possibility of discharging your loved one on Monday, ask them what they plan to do over the weekend. If they state they simply want to watch your loved one, ask if you can't do the same at home.

The only good thing that happened as a result of the nights, weekends, and holiday syndrome was that, on the Mother's Day mentioned above, I was able to sneak our 75-pound Rhodesian Ridgeback dog into Bill's hospital room, with the full permission of the nurse in charge. Pet therapy is a wonderful thing. Bill had been denied access to the four-legged members of his family for more than seven months at that time, and the clandestine canine visit truly helped his mood. Precisely because of the absence of staff, this nurse felt less vulnerable should I have gotten caught.

I would have traded this visit in a heartbeat, however, for competent and consistent care during the eight and a-half months of nights, weekends, and holidays we spent in hospitals.

24/7 or Dead

Don't let the bad thing called nights, weekends, and holidays cost you the life of your loved one! If you are forced to remain in the hospital during these times, adopt the posture humorously defined in this statement: *I'm not tense, just terribly, terribly alert.*

CHAPTER 6
Execute a Durable Medical Power of Attorney, a Living Will and a Power of Attorney

"It's been emphatically proven that even seeds that appear dead–that is to say, were incapable of bearing life–for thousands of years, because of the conditions in which they were kept, can, given the appropriate conditions, suddenly bloom. So surely our history is like those seeds. The question is, how can they be activated? Under what circumstances? In whom? Where? What makes us able to live can only happen– and we can advance–with access to the past."

—Vanessa Redgrave, *Interview – April, 1997*

RECOMMENDATION #4: EXECUTE A DURABLE MEDICAL POWER OF ATTORNEY, A LIVING WILL AND A POWER OF ATTORNEY. No one can tell you what is going to happen and this is especially true when

you are messing with the human body. No two bodies are the same. The same procedure can go perfectly 200 times and the 201st time, everything can go wrong.

Talk about a case of the cobbler's children not having shoes! I was married to an attorney, who refused to deal with legal issues such as powers of attorney and living wills because "it was too upsetting to think about them." Therefore, I entered this medical nightmare as "just a spouse," not as a person who had Durable Medical Power of Attorney. There is a **big** difference!

Let's be clear about terms. A Durable Medical Power of Attorney specifically states that a designated person has the legal right to make healthcare decisions for another, should the other become incapacitated. A Living Will specifies extraordinary efforts **not** be used to prolong my life should I become terminally ill. Both documents plus a third, a Power of Attorney that specifies the legal right to make any decision for an incapacitated person, are necessary.

Be advised that some states include the Living Will within the Durable Medical Power of Attorney, making this an all-inclusive document. Legal advisors and advocacy offices will be able to direct you in this matter.

Execute Legal Documents

I separate the Durable Medical Power of Attorney from the Power of Attorney for simplicity when dealing with the healthcare community.

Seeds planted many months before caused us to need a Durable Medical Power of Attorney. Because of my desire to understand what was going on with Bill, I had asked for and received an excellent education regarding the review of lab results. Additionally, I had done extensive research on each organ failure and disease process attributed to Bill. Therefore, I was probably asked almost daily what kind of medical training I had received. My response was usually, "24/7 since October 23, 2000" (the date of Bill's admission to the hospital).

That statement wasn't entirely true. I did a lot of research (see Chapter 9), I asked a lot of questions, and I listened like a hawk anytime anyone was discussing Bill's condition. I listened so closely I was, at one time, asked to step away from the consult table so the doctors and nurses could speak freely among themselves. I honored that doctor's request on the condition he share the gist of their discussion. As I've mentioned earlier, I had also received basic and advanced first aid training and Emergency Medical Technician (EMT) training earlier in my career. Additionally, this was my husband, after all, and I wanted in on the discussions.

It has been my experience that you run into two types of healthcare providers:

- those who appreciate your knowledge and wish to partner with you and
- those who do not.

The real need for a Durable Medical Power of Attorney occurs when you deal with the latter.

While we were at Hospital #2, the healthcare providers denied my repeated requests to see Bill's lab results for five days. When I would sneak a look at his labs on the table outside his room, someone would always come over and remove them from the table. During that time, I progressively worked my way up the hospital administrative ladder until I finally reached the Patient Rights folks. I now know to start there, but since they were previously unknown to me (I was unaware of the existence of such at Hospital #1 and, frankly, did not need them), I had to discover their existence on my own.

It took a ninety-minute meeting between the doctor in charge of the ICU at Hospital #2 and the Patient Rights advocates to convince the doctor I had a right to see this information, even though the hospital's Patient Rights Statement clearly specified such a right.

In responding to my request, the doctor commented that it was "unusual for a family member to want the depth of information" I sought. I found this statement questionable since this facility was world-renowned and most patients and family members who sought treatment there were well educated about the presenting condition and arrived seeking alternatives.

In any case, although they granted me the right to see this information, they required that a doctor be present while I looked at it so he or she could explain what I did not understand. Even after this commitment, if I did not remind them of my desire to see the labs, they failed to make arrangements to meet with me. After another five frustrating days of reminders, I asked that they set a specific time to review the lab results with me. It was only on the last day of Bill's hospital stay there that they shared the lab results with me in a timely fashion.

I experienced this same frustration at Hospital #3, albeit not at the same level, since we were back with the same doctors who had been treating Bill at Hospital #1. I was denied lab result access upon entry at Hospital #4, as well. Therefore, when Bill was finally mentally competent, I asked his friend, Skip (who's also an attorney) to draft both a Durable Medical Power of Attorney and a Living Will. I presented them to Bill, stating I thought we were past the point where we really needed these but I didn't want to take any chances. Bill made minor revisions to Skip's documents and we both cried as we executed them in front of witnesses. I then contacted the legal department in the hospital and one of the attorneys came up to Bill's room and accepted service (officially received and acknowledged receipt) of the documents. I kept a copy of both documents and placed them in my purse.

Less than three weeks later, Bill coded, going back into Medical ICU on full life support. Because of the unknown duration of the seizures and stroke that put him there, we did not know what mental condition he would be in when he finally woke up. It was the first time I considered there might be a need for a Living Will. From this point forward, anytime anyone denied me information, I produced my copy of the Durable Medical Power of Attorney and that resolved the issue. How I wish we had executed one prior to Bill's admission to Hospital #1.

There were other problems, too. For example, I discovered the paperwork, when transferring Bill from one part of the hospital to another, was problematic. A patient with either or both of these documents in all four hospitals had a stamp on the front of their file indicating the existence of such. However, when Bill was transferred, the stamp, and frequently the document, did not follow and I would once again have to produce my copy.

If you do not have easy or free access to an attorney, the legal office of any hospital should be able to provide you with sample documents at no charge. I recommend you execute multiple originals of both a Durable Medical Power of Attorney and a Living Will prior to admission to the hospital. When your family member is admitted, produce an original of each document and ask to receive an acknowledgement (proof of service document) indicating the hospital's receipt of both documents.

God forbid that Bill ends up sick again, since I still do not have a Power of Attorney document that allows me to make all decisions governing property, money, etc., in the case of incapacity. I am working on this with the cobbler.

In the Appendix you will find a sample of each of these documents. Please do not copy these and expect them to comply with your state laws. Each state requires different things on the form. You *must* get some type of legal advice on these documents, if just from the hospital.

A final word about Patient Rights and the Psychiatric Unit. At one point in Bill's recovery, he voluntarily committed himself to the Psychiatric Unit of Hospital #4. This occurred because of the mix of stroke damage and medication complications. Both his psychiatrist and I believed it would be best to try a new medication under the watchful eyes of specialists. Be advised that the rules are very different in a Psychiatric Unit. Hospitals use the term, "lock-up" to refer to the method they used to ensure patient safety in a Psychiatric Unit. Does that give you a hint as to how Patient Rights are viewed in such a setting?

Execute Legal Documents

CHECKLIST E—Required Documents

ACTIONS FOR YOU TO TAKE	√
Obtain a sample Durable Medical Power of Attorney	
Make revisions to the Durable Medical Power of Attorney only with appropriate counsel	
Type (word process) and execute at least three copies	
Place one copy in the hands of the admitting hospital, one copy in the hands of the Patient Rights advocate, and one copy in safekeeping (safety deposit box, fire proof vault, etc.)	
Receive proof of service acknowledgement from hospital and place in safekeeping	
Obtain a sample Living Will	
Make revisions to the Living Will only with appropriate counsel	
Type (word process) and execute at least three copies	
Place one copy in the hands of the admitting hospital, one copy in the hands of the Patient Rights advocate, and one copy in safekeeping (safety deposit box, fire proof vault, etc.)	
Receive proof of service acknowledgement from hospital and place in safekeeping	
Obtain a sample Power of Attorney	
Make revisions to the Power of Attorney only with appropriate counsel	
Type (word process) and execute at least three copies	

ACTIONS FOR YOU TO TAKE	√
Place one copy in the hands of your attorney or the executor of your estate, one copy with your will, and one copy in safekeeping (safety deposit box, fire proof vault, etc.)	
Receive proof of service acknowledgement from the hospital attorney and place in safekeeping	

CHAPTER 7
Read and Use the Patient Rights Statement

With a stout heart, a mouse can lift an elephant.
—Tibetan Proverb, *A World Treasury*

RECOMMENDATION #5: READ AND USE THE PATIENT RIGHTS STATEMENT. Repeat it back to the hospital and the healthcare providers anytime they resist your questions or involvement. This is particularly true when you have a Durable Medical Power of Attorney. Ask what the rules are and challenge any that don't make sense to you.

Before we can deal with the concept of Patient Rights, we must first make your family member a patient, rather than a disease, a condition or a body part. In order to do this, bring in photographs of your family member and paste them on the doors, windows, or walls of the hospital room. This makes the patient "real" to the doctors and nurses.

- real in that they look healthy in the pictures, so there is a goal
- real in that the patient has children, a spouse, parents, friends
- real in that this person has a life to which he or she wants to return

I posted pictures on Bill's door so care providers could see what my husband looked like vertical! Although it was a joke, those pictures represented a defining moment—this unconscious patient became a real human being to these people. Then, and only then, could I begin to deal with Bill's and my rights.

In the era of the caveman, which caveman got the prettiest mate? The one with the most muscle! The one with the most muscle cultivated the biggest army, acquired the most powerful weapon, and possessed the greatest desire to conquer. Muscle equaled power.

In the era of European landed gentry, who had the most power? Those who owned the land. In the decade of the 1980s, who

Read and Use the Patient Rights Statement

had the most power? The moneyed. They ruled with wealth. In our very recent history, however, what has happened to the Donald Trumps of the world? They lost money. Why? There was a shift in power currency.

The shift is toward a new basis for power: information. How did the Japanese gain such an early and large portion of the computer industry? They used information to overpower us – information we provided to them! How have many companies, such as Enron, maintained control over their employees? By withholding information. The same technique has been adopted by some of our healthcare providers.

In the prior chapter, I identified the two types of healthcare providers I experienced during this horrifying ordeal:

- those who appreciate your knowledge and wish to partner with you; and
- those who do not.

There is a strong push in this country for Patient Rights, a movement that was started to combat the healthcare providers who neither appreciate our knowledge nor wish to partner with us. (This is not limited to healthcare providers. I have had the same experience with insurance carriers, hospital administrators and others.) The next step beyond the assumption that my knowledge is irrelevant is that I must be controlled. In order to control me, rules (laws) must be in place so I can be controlled (denied information or given only what the provider wants me to have). Since we live in the age where information is power, being denied or provided only limited information strips me of the ability to advocate on behalf of my loved one. This is not acceptable!

In the Appendix you will find a sample Patient Advocacy Statement (sometimes called a Patient Rights Statement). Your hospital's Patient Advocacy Statement will look similar. Several aspects of this statement bear scrutiny.

Patient Rights

- Appoint a surrogate to make healthcare decisions on your behalf to the extent permitted by law.

- Understandable information concerning diagnosis, treatment and prognosis, and financial implications of treatment choices.

- Involvement in medical decision-making, including refusal of care and treatment, to the extent permitted by law, and being informed of the medical consequences of refusal.

- Reasonable access to review medical records pertaining to your care, and to receive copies of these records for a reasonable photocopying fee.

- Be informed of and participate in treatment decisions and the care planning process.

- Be informed of hospital policies and resources, such as Patient Rights advocates and the ethics committee.

- Expect a reasonable response to your need/request for assistance in effective communication, regardless of language or disability.

Of the twenty-nine issues provided in the sample Patient Advocacy Statement, seven deal with being provided adequate information to participate as a partner in your family member's healthcare. This represents 20 percent of the statement, a percentage larger than any other single theme. Since it is reasonable to believe an attorney crafted these statements, why do you think this theme is so prevalent?

Being married to an attorney, I posed this question to Bill. His reply was, "Rules are generally made in response to litigation." What does this tell you? It says to me these statements were crafted as a result of patients and family members being denied access and ultimately suing a hospital. Although disguised as

Patient Rights, these rules are written for healthcare providers to reduce the likelihood of a lawsuit.

Don't be fooled, however. Just because the rules are written doesn't mean you'll find compliance in all cases. Here are some examples of my experiences in this area.

- Not one of the four hospitals informed me of the in-hospital library available to me for research (*be informed of hospital resources*), although I ultimately used all four of them.

- Hospital #2 administered Haldol (a very powerful psychotropic drug) to Bill against my stated objection (*be informed of and participate in treatment decisions* **and** *involvement in medical decision-making including refusal of care and treatment*). When I objected a second time, they asked the Psychiatric Department Chair to come and talk to me. When she arrived, she spent her entire visit attempting to get Bill's mother and me to discuss how we were feeling and what we were doing to care for ourselves. Although this conversation may have been appropriate in another setting, what did it have to do with Bill taking Haldol? It was merely another effort to distract and control.

- I have mentioned the consistent denial to hospital records (*reasonable access to review the medical records*).

- Not one of the four hospitals informed me about the availability of Patient Rights advocates (*be informed of hospital policies and resources, such as Patient Rights advocates*) or the right to challenge hospital employees' actions (*access an internal grievance process and appeal to an external agency*). As a result, I almost lost unrestricted access to Bill. At one point in time at Hospital #4, a contract nurse (a nurse who did not work for the hospital but for an employment agency that supplies temporary help to the hospital) as well as the head nurse of the same unit denied me access to information and routinely asked me to leave the room during their treatments. Bill was in the Medical ICU after his fourth code. This was six months into his hospital stay and, by this time, I was well informed and quite knowledgeable, not only about his case but about the equipment being used to treat his various conditions. The nurses and respiratory therapists frequently asked me to assist with his care so, when the ventilator alarm went off and a nurse was not forthcoming, I would do what the hospital staff had trained me to do. I silenced the alarm (this only shuts it off for a short time), pressed the nurse call button, and then went to find the nurse or respiratory therapist. Remember, this is in the ICU. Please note slow response occurs here as well. I had done this very thing possibly thirty times in the past with no consequence.

On one particular day, the respiratory therapist assigned to Bill witnessed me silencing the alarm (I had a headache and it had been chiming loudly for more than three minutes without response—good thing Bill wasn't dying!). Upon entering the room, she announced that was responsible for responding to the alarm and managing the ventilator (both true statements) and I was not to touch it. I responded by citing the thirty or more times I had done this very thing in the past. She said she didn't care; I was **not** to touch the ventilator. I later learned she left the room and reported me to the head nurse.

The next day, Bill had a very efficient and friendly nurse caring for him. During one visit where I was helping her change the bedding, the ventilator alarm went off (as it frequently does when you alter airway access during a patient roll) and she asked me to silence it. Since I was on the side of the bed with the ventilator, I reached over and shut off the alarm.

Read and Use the Patient Rights Statement

If you were standing outside Bill's room, you could see the ventilator and me fully but would not be able to see the nurse without entering the room. Apparently someone saw me touch the ventilator and reported it to the head nurse. He came into the room, asked me to leave and wait in an adjacent "quiet room" (a room provided in some hospitals for family members to use). I waited, with my mother-in-law (who had witnessed everything) at my side, and about an hour later, the head nurse entered the room and told me that because I was "intentionally interfering with my husband's treatment" (touching the ventilator), I was going to be denied access to his room and only allowed in when someone on staff was present to monitor my activities.

This occurred during a time when I was very frightened and exhausted, so I really didn't know what to do. A respiratory therapist (Lee) who had cared for Bill in Hospital #1 had just arrived on the scene, and when I told her what had happened, she was appalled.

She called a nurse colleague, who was one of the two nurses who had been with Bill the most during his stay in Hospital #1, and who had become a friend by this time. Rebecca came to my rescue.

Upon arrival at the hospital, she went straight to the Patient Advocacy office and asked for an immediate hearing. So, while I am crying in the hallway of the MICU and unable to enter Bill's room, hospital employees meet without me to prepare for my "hearing" in a nearby conference room. The hospital representatives included a Patient Rights advocate, the MICU head nurse, a social worker, and an attorney for the hospital. When I was finally invited to join them, I brought my mother-in-law, Lee, and Rebecca for support.

The hearing started with the head nurse levelly his charge of me "intentionally interfering with the treatment of my husband." Whenever I tried to respond to his statements, he silenced me, until even the other meeting participants asked him to remain silent while I told my side of the story.

During the course of the hour-long meeting, I was finally able to explain what happened and ask whether the head nurse had talked to the nurse present when I silenced the alarm (he had not). Lee, Rebecca, and my mother-in-law told the group how strongly I had been advocating for Bill and how eager I was to learn what was going on and about the necessary equipment so I

Read and Use the Patient Rights Statement

could help. They stated in no uncertain terms that I had never interfered with Bill's treatment.

It was interesting to watch the reactions when the participants learned what Bill and I had been through. However, even at this point, there was no indication I would be allowed unrestricted access.

At Rebecca's urging, I pulled out my trump cards, threatening that if the hospital denied me access to Bill, I would have to consider a malpractice suit against the hospital. Boy, did that get their attention! All of a sudden, the heretofore silent attorney sat up straighter, asked me what I meant, and started taking copious notes.

I described the time when Bill was dropped during a transfer and a tube was pulled out, requiring the chief thoracic surgeon of the hospital to respond on a run to the nurse's emergency page. I also told about the ICU incident where the monitor had been mis-set (the alarm settings were too high), and I had to alert the nurse that Bill was in sinus ventricular tachachardia (SVT). It was amazing how quickly after that I was again allowed unrestricted access. I eventually found out the MICU head nurse was demoted as a result of this incident.

It is important to note several things about this incident. First, the hospital staff stuck together. Second, I would not have known about the transfer drop or the mis-set monitor had I not been present 24/7. And third, had Rebecca not known about the Patient Rights advocate, I would have lost unrestricted access for the last 2+ months Bill was hospitalized.

I received a visit from all involved in the hearing following the event, each of them apologizing for the way things were handled. Was this true remorse or lawsuit prevention? I will never know. All that mattered was that I was allowed access to Bill.

Being an Advocate

As an advocate for a loved one, we become the ones responsible for compliance with the hospital rules. Sometimes, when we believe we are being denied information, we must become the "pain-in-the-ass family member" (a name that was frequently applied to me, supposedly out of my earshot). There are five issues for us to confront in this role.

- Widespread reluctance to engage in conflict.

- Lack of knowledge and, therefore, failure to ask the right questions.

- Doctors and nurses, because of their workload, are disinclined to spend precious time answering all your questions.

- Many doctors are specialists and only look at their designated body part. Therefore, they become uncomfortable when we ask about how treatments and side effects will affect other parts of the patient.

- Many doctors, although they are gifted technicians, have difficulty communicating, especially with frightened and demanding family members.

If you want and/or need to be the advocate for your loved one, you either have to speak up or get help. Otherwise, you may lose your loved one on your watch.

Other issues contained within the *Patient Rights* portion of the Patient Advocacy Statement include:

- *Be free from restraints or seclusion, imposed as a means of coercion, discipline, convenience or retaliation by staff.* All of the hospitals we were involved with were careful with this one. As mentioned, at one point Bill needed to be restrained as he was confused and frequently pulled out tubes. All the nursing staffs were very diligent about discussing this with me.

- *Confidentiality of information.* Sometimes I felt the care providers were attempting to keep Bill's condition and medical information confidential from me! One hospital employee even said as much to me.

- *Decline participation in experimental treatments.* In Hospital #4, there was an experiment going on regarding a new protocol for treating bedsores. I was asked if I wanted Bill to participate in the experiment or simply try the new treatment. I chose the latter.

Remember, Patient Rights Statement are written by attorneys to protect hospitals. They *are not* written to protect patients' rights. So we must fight for that. Consider writing your congressional representatives to advocate for a National Patient Bill of Rights.

In the name of patient protection, an addition was recently added to the Health Insurance Portability and Accountability Act of 1996, affectionately called HIPAA. This law was passed for two primary reasons:

- to standardize the treatment of patient confidentiality that previously differed from state to state; and ultimately,

- to inspire patient confidence about the way health information is stored and maintained throughout the industry.

Why would the healthcare industry not try to block this kind of regulation? To the extent patients are comfortable about the measures implemented to protect sensitive health information, "the expectation is the industry will be in a better position to take advantage of technological innovations like computerized patient records that allow for greater efficiency and accuracy in the provision of care" (read: increase profits due to more efficiencies).

Additionally, the Health and Human Services Agency, which is responsible for enforcing the privacy rule, has stated investigations will be complaint-driven and emphasize voluntary resolutions to problems. According to Richard M. Campanelli, director of the Office for Civil Rights, HIPAA violators will be "engage[d] to achieve voluntary resolution" of compliance failures and if resolved, "that is likely to be the end of it."

Fines will be imposed only in those cases where a covered entity does not make a "good faith" effort to correct violations of the privacy rule.

And last, this law defines the benchmark not just for compliance with the privacy rule, but in any instances where patient confidentiality is at issue. Although the intent is laudable, I fear the outcome may create even greater difficulty in accessing your loved one's medical information.

This law strives to protect how medical information about a patient may be used and disclosed and how the patient can get access to this information. As with many new laws, I predict it will be accompanied by confusion, mistakes, and myriad problems no one anticipated.

Notice of Privacy Practices

The Appendix contains a sample Notice of Privacy Practices. The one for your hospital will look similar. Like the Patient Advocacy Statement, several aspects of this statement bear scrutiny. Unlike the Patient Advocacy Statement, these governing practices were enacted after Bill's hospitalization.

My primary concern with this addition to the Health Insurance Portability and Accountability Act of 1996 (HIPAA) deals with the possibility of restricted information to you, the family member. I had to fight hard, especially in Hospital #2, to get even the most basic information about Bill's condition. Even when I prevailed, the hospital stalled in providing the information.

Read and Use the Patient Rights Statement

If I had this kind of difficulty without the presence of these supposed protections, what might I expect today?

Here are the specific statements in the *Notice of Privacy Practices* that concern me regarding the ability to freely access information about a family member. Pay particular attention to the information I have highlighted in **bold** print:

- *We **may** disclose medical information about you to a friend or family member who is involved in your care.*

- *Unless you object, we **may** disclose medical information about you to a friend or family member who is involved in your medical care and we may disclose medical information about you to an entity assisting in a disaster relief effort so that your family can be notified about your location and condition.*

- *If you are not present or able to object, then we **may**, using our professional judgment, determine whether the disclosure is in your best interest.*

This language makes it even more imperative that your loved one provide an executed Durable Medical Power of Attorney prior to hospitalization.

Another issue of concern relates to access to medical information used to make decisions about patient care. As stated before, I had tremendous difficulty with Hospital #2 in being allowed to see Bill's X-rays and CT scans. Although the following statement says the *patient* has the right to see such records, it is silent regarding the family members:

- *Right to Inspect and Copy. You have the right to inspect and have copied medical information used to make decisions about your care. Usually, this includes medical and billing records, but does not include some records such as psychotherapy notes.*

Prior to leaving Hospital #2, I requested that the hospital forward a copy of Bill's X-rays and CT scans to me so I could share them with Hospital #3. The requested films did not show up until well into Bill's stay at Hospital #4—five months after the request and discharge from Hospital #2. Clearly, this made it impossible for both Hospital #3 and Hospital #4 to use these films as a baseline for his condition.

The following statement is silent on timeliness:

- *To inspect and have copied medical information used to make decisions about you, you must submit your request in writing. Call Release of Information at XXXX*

Read and Use the Patient Rights Statement for further details. We may charge a fee for the costs of processing your request.

One of the most upsetting decisions made by three of the four hospitals involved release of information to a *former* family member. I requested Bill's condition and treatments specifically **not** be released to this former family member who had frequently called Hospital #1 and occupied Bill's nurse on the phone for up to twenty minutes, during one of the most critical periods of his illness.

I spoke with this individual several times, as did other family members, requesting that she contact someone from the family for an update. When she consistently failed to do so and continued to place phone calls that caused the nurse in charge of Bill's care to stop treating him and speak instead with her, I asked the hospital to refuse to provide such information to her, since she had no legal right to it. This person "pretended to be someone else on the phone" (as reported by one of the nurses who took her call) and ultimately threatened lawsuits for failure to provide relevant information to her.

Three of the four hospitals capitulated in the face of a threatened but groundless lawsuit, and provided whatever data she requested. Remember, this is *not* a family member! It wasn't until we got to the fourth hospital that she was told no information would be forthcoming and she could file suit against the hospital if she chose.

In this case, I do believe the Notice of Privacy Practices would have been helpful in disallowing the first three hospitals from releasing information. However, I can't be sure, since the law only allows the **patient** to stop the information flow. Also, note the statement in **bold** that clearly allows the hospital to make its own judgment call regarding this issue.

- *Right To Request Restrictions. You have the right to request a restriction or limitation on the medical information we use or disclose about you for treatment, payment or healthcare operations. You also have the right to request a limit on the medical information we disclose about you to someone who is involved in your care or in the payment for your care, like a family member or friend.* ***We are not required to agree to your request.*** *If we do agree, we will comply with your request unless the information is needed to provide you emergency treatment.*

Bottom line, patient treatment information is getting harder to access without legal authority. You must play by the rules since this access is now federally mandated. The Patient Rights office and/or legal counsel may be able to assist you if you

Read and Use the Patient Rights Statement

are without a Durable Medical Power of Attorney. If you must fight, remember this quote by Helen Keller:

*I am only one; but still I am one.
I cannot do everything, but still I can do something;
I will not refuse to do something I can do.*

CHAPTER 8
Assume Your Loved One Can Hear Everything So Phrase Everything in the Positive

A group of frogs was traveling through the woods, and two of them fell into a deep pit. All the other frogs gathered around the pit. When they saw how deep the pit was, they told the unfortunate frogs they would never get out. The two frogs ignored the comments and tried to jump up out of the pit. The other frogs kept telling them to stop, that they were as good as dead. Finally, one of the frogs took heed to what the other frogs were saying and simply gave up. He fell down and died.

The other frog continued to jump as hard as he could. Once again, the crowd of frogs yelled at him to stop the pain and suffering and just die. He jumped even harder and finally made it out.

When he got out, the other frogs asked him, "Why did you continue jumping? Didn't you hear us?"

The frog explained to them that he was deaf. He thought they were encouraging him the entire time.

This story teaches two lessons:
1. There is power of life and death in the tongue. An encouraging word to someone who is down can lift them up and help them make it through the day.
2. A destructive word to someone who is down can be what it takes to kill them.
Be careful of what you say.
Speak life to those who cross your path.

—Author Unknown

RECOMMENDATION #6: ASSUME YOUR LOVED ONE CAN HEAR EVERYTHING SO PHRASE EVERYTHING IN THE POSITIVE. We are told people in a coma can hear what we say, even if they cannot respond. Having an upsetting conversation with doctors or family members in the presence of your loved one, even when they are heavily sedated, can have extremely negative consequences. So can whispering when the patient believes something is being withheld.

The universe (God) is always attentive to our requests. The universe (God) listens and responds to our requests. The universe (God) doesn't understand statements made in the negative. "Heal my husband" is a clear request. "Don't let my husband get sicker" is heard as "Let my husband get sicker". State everything in the positive.

According to Rick Work in his book, *Awaken to the Healer Within*, there are universal laws that govern all creation. Here are the first two:

Reprinted with permission

The Law of Magnetic Attraction

You attract to you that which you desire. You also attract to you that which you do not desire–if you focus on it. If you focus on disease, you will manifest more disease. If you focus on poverty, you will manifest more poverty. If you focus on the lack of love in your life, you will only manifest more lack. It is not possible to create love when you focus on fear. It is not possible to create prosperity when you focus on poverty. That is the Law of Magnetic Attraction.

The Law of Creative Manifestation

Now that you understand law #1, invoke law #2. Intentionally focus on that which you desire. And, do not focus on that which you do not desire in your life. If you are in a room where others are engaged in a conversation about something that you do not desire, politely excuse yourself and leave. To remain in that energy will only attract more of it into your life.

A third law will be discussed in Chapter 15.

What all of these quotations and all of our experience shows is **Bill heard everything!** The sensitive doctors had discussions about his condition outside the room. The insensitive ones began discussions in his room. If the topic was negative and I was present, I immediately asked them to move the discussion outside the room.

Those who saw me as a partner complied. Those who did not usually replied with a statement like, "Your husband has a right to hear about his condition." While I agreed in theory, telling a person anesthetized into unconsciousness and critically ill that his chance of surviving surgery is less than 5 percent is not helpful.

Bill returned from a two-week visit to his mom's home in Florida early in his recovery. During the trip, he and his mom discussed his hospitalization in detail, and as a result of some of their discussions, he came home with the statement, "I think I heard my mom when I was unconscious in the hospital."

This statement came nine months after discharge. Whether this is actually true or he wishes it so, the fact is his mother and I constantly said positive things to him while he was hospitalized. Every day, I wrote and posted a positive affirmation on the wall for him to see. I wrote such things as, "My kidneys are healthy" and "I can and will walk up and down the hall today."

Bill's primary in-hospital physical therapist, Lori, wrote affirmations and posted progress charts for him to see. During his crucial septic episodes, all involved would hold his hand and tell him how much we wanted him to stay. Even though he was unconscious during his sepsis, he must have heard us and chosen to stay since he survived.

Every time some negative statement or a negative event occurred in his room or within his hearing, he had a setback. Twice I got into heated discussions with doctors in his room (I was tired and didn't think to move the discussion into the hall), and both times Bill had physical or mental setbacks following the discussions.

I learned from my friend Jean, a Reiki therapist who did energy work with Bill, the universe hears things differently than we speak them. If we say, "I don't want to feel pain today," the universe translates this into "I feel pain today." Negatives don't register, so why use them? State everything in the positive, as if it were so. The universe will respond and align the words and the wish, as when Captain Picard of the starship Enterprise would say, "Make it so!" and Wesley Crusher would promptly comply.

Many books and card decks are available that contain affirmations. If you cannot think of any specific affirmations for your situation, get one of these tools from your local bookstore or library and use the relevant affirmations. There are also sites on the Internet that offer health-related affirmations, some very specific to the condition(s) of your loved one. Using an affirmation is much like a psychologist telling you to "act as if and it will become so." Change starts inside.

By saying things like —

- I have the power to control my health
- I am in control of my health and wellness
- I have abundant energy, vitality and well-being
- I am healthy in all aspects of my being

we begin to affect the behavior, and eventually it affects the body or the outer packaging.

If you create a positive environment for healing, healing is much more likely to occur. As Mahatma Gandhi said,

Be the change you want to see in the world.

CHAPTER 9
Educate Yourself

The real voyage of discovery consists not in seeking new landscapes, but in having new eyes.

—Marcel Proust

RECOMMENDATION #7: EDUCATE YOURSELF. Learn everything you can about the illness, disease or injury being treated and about the equipment being used to provide treatment. The more you know, the more you can help the healthcare providers, even when they do not want your help.

Rule #1: Equipment = tool.

Use of equipment has dramatically improved healthcare in the last twenty years. However, many healthcare

professionals rely so heavily on equipment, they fail to look at the patient.

Rule #2: When in doubt, look at the patient.

Once we begin to state everything in the positive, we can learn about the challenge facing us and our loved one. We can learn about the illness, disease, or injury. Understanding and attitude are everything. A story being passed around the Internet illustrates this important connection:

Many years ago, when I worked as a volunteer at a hospital, I got to know a little girl named Liz, who was suffering from a rare and serious disease. Her only chance of recovery appeared to be a blood transfusion from her five-year-old brother, who had miraculously survived the same disease and had developed the antibodies needed to combat the illness.

The doctor explained the situation to her little brother, and asked the little boy if he would be willing to give his blood to his sister. I saw him hesitate for only a moment before taking a deep breath and saying, "Yes, I'll do it if it will save her."

As the transfusion progressed, he lay in bed next to his sister and smiled, as we all did, seeing the color returning to her cheeks. Then his face grew pale and his smile faded. He looked up at the doctor and asked with a trembling voice, "Will I start to die right away?"

Being young, the little boy had misunderstood the doctor; he thought he was going to have to give his sister all of his blood in order to save her. You see, after all, understanding and attitude are everything.

So, let's learn! Start with the obvious—learn the names of your care providers. I found the nurses to be especially grateful for small favors such as cookies, candy, and doughnuts. Establishing relationships with care providers clearly makes them more willing to help you.

Ask them questions about everything! If you ask it in a respectful tone, they are more likely to respond. For example, "Can you help me understand?" served me well. I kept a notebook with me at all times and wrote down the information I received and who said it. Then, when I had to ask questions of another doctor, I could quote both the statement and the source from a prior discussion. Be aware, there will be days when either the doctors won't have time to talk or won't want to talk. In such cases, see if they can either tell you when they will have time or if they can provide another source, such as a resident or a medical student. Don't take no for an answer. Not only do you have a right to know what is going on and to understand the treatment to the best of your ability, you are paying for the service! The doctors and nurses work for you and your loved one. They are not doing you a favor! Remember, the Patient Advocacy Statement says you are entitled to *"Understandable information concerning diagnosis, treatment and prognosis, and financial implications of treatment choices."*

Another source is the hospital library. All hospitals have one, even though you may have to ask for its location. As with any library, some books may be removed and others may not. If a book cannot be removed, make copies of the relevant articles. Most hospital libraries allow a certain number of free copies before they began to charge. Also, if you lack computer access to search the Internet, for example, some medical libraries may grant you online access as well as assist you with your search. This is more likely in a teaching or university hospital library, and less likely in a private hospital library. Regardless, it doesn't hurt to ask.

The third source of information is the Internet. Because the Internet is not regulated, you may come across information that is inaccurate and potentially harmful. Fortunately, I did not experience this. What I did find was the most current, up-to-date information and protocols regarding Bill's multiple medical conditions. Some of the material I discovered was so good the doctors asked for copies of the articles!

A little known source of information is the literature available on the hospital floor. In Hospital #1, I found an exhaustive nurse's text that provided me with loads of information on care and disease. On every floor of every hospital we were in, I found a Physician's Desk Reference or PDR, which details drugs, their purposes, and their side effects. I can't tell you how many nights I went to the PDR to read about new medications prescribed for Bill. Did I understand all the technical language? Not a chance!

However, I did glean enough information to discuss my support or concern with the doctors the following day during their rounds. *The Pill Book*, or any similar yearly published drug reference guide, will serve the same purpose.

My main concern was the impact of medications on Bill's kidneys. I always looked at the contraindications of specific medications. I also looked at what organs were involved in the breakdown of each medicine as well as drug interactions. On several occasions, I discussed kidney involvement in drug processing and asked doctors to consider alternate medications. Know where your loved one is most vulnerable and focus your efforts there in the beginning. You can then expand your field of focus.

Despite my eagerness to learn, I was often frightened by my research. When an article described the progression of acute pancreatitis and offered survival rates based on factors, I assessed the factors against Bill's condition. More often than not, they would point to his death. Although this scared me, at least I understood the extent of his illness. As a result of gaining this information, I increased the frequency and intensity of my prayers.

With regard to your loved one's illness, disease, or injury, ignorance is not bliss. This labor is a reminder that anything I can face, I can handle. Arming yourself with knowledge is an indication you are willing to advocate for your loved one. This is especially critical in the "body part specialty" hospitals (teaching or university hospitals) where you have to be the one who pays attention to the whole patient.

In addition to learning about the illness, disease, or injury your loved one is experiencing, learn about the equipment used in treatment. According to a Chinese proverb, *"The beginning of wisdom is to recall things by their right names."* For example, if an alarm is going off and you need to notify someone, the staff will not understand the importance of their response if you don't use the right terms.

Unless you have been trained in medicine, **now** is the time to begin your education! You will get little credibility from the physicians if you cannot speak their language. If you can speak their language, even just a little, doors will open—with the doctors, with the nurses, and with your loved one, who will want to understand what is happening or what has happened to him or her.

The Navajo say, *"Bless those who challenge us to grow, to stretch, to move beyond the knowable, to come back home to our essential, elemental nature. Bless those who challenge us for they remind us of doors we have closed and doors we have yet to open. They are big medicine teachers for us."* Another way of looking at this is to be grateful for all the challenging people in your life—bosses, co-workers, in-laws, children, and friends, because they're your greatest teachers.

These relationships are difficult precisely because of your resistance to the lesson, which might be about compassion, self-worth, generosity, or unconditional love. Failing to advocate is more about you than your loved one. Who would have thought someone else's illness, disease or injury would be "big medicine" for us?

CHAPTER 10

Ask About Every Medication, Injection or Intravenous Solution Used or Denied in Treatment

When we try to pick out anything by itself, we find it hitched to everything else in the universe.

—John Muir

RECOMMENDATION #8: ASK ABOUT EVERY MEDICATION, INJECTION OR INTRAVENOUS SOLUTION USED OR DENIED IN TREATMENT. Each medication has side effects, as television commercials so pointedly illustrate.

The five rules for the correct administration of drugs are:

- right patient
- right drug

- right dose
- right route
- right time

In order to ensure that the right patient receives the right drug, those who administer drugs ought to check the patient wristbands (name and allergies) before administering any drug. This does not always happen and can lead to mistakes. Let's make it harder to make a mistake!

The simple practice of writing:

- a patient's name
- room number
- bed number (if the room is shared)
- allergies
- chronic conditions
- impairments (such as sight or hearing)

on a big piece of paper or poster board and taping it over the patient's bed is something we can do to move the odds in our family member's favor. This is especially important if your family member is unconscious.

Intravenous Solutions

Administration of intravenous solutions to dehydrated or undernourished patients is considered a fairly routine practice in hospitals. There is nothing routine about this practice! I mentioned in Chapter 2 how Bill experienced thirteen septic episodes. With the exception of one, they were all the result of intravenous line infections. Let me be clear, Bill was critically ill and much more susceptible to this type of infection. Also, keep in mind the probability of an infection is higher in Intensive Care because the patients are sicker. However, every time the hospital "punches a hole" in your loved one, the possibility of infection increases. Infection occurs by introducing an avenue for the stuff on the outside of the body to get into the inside of the body where it doesn't belong.

Here is how this works. We all have invisible intruders living on our skin. On the outside of the body, they do little harm. However, when you open a clear path to the inside of the body (an IV line) **and** they find their way in (sometimes during the actual needle punch, sometimes due to sloppy line maintenance, sometimes through who knows how), they do dastardly damage to our innards. When an IV line gets infected, the bad guys get introduced into the bloodstream and are carried to all parts of the body. This causes sepsis, characterized by a raging fever, low blood pressure, and increased respiration. Toxic shock syndrome, caused by wearing tampons for too long, is a recognized form of sepsis.

Sepsis is life-threatening! Bill had two particularly bad episodes where his blood pressure hovered at 60/30 for four hours each time, during which he had at least one heart attack and one stroke. He still suffers the consequences of those episodes today.

Having said all this and scared you to death, I am not saying you should stop the administration of IV fluids. What I am saying is that **you,** the advocate, must keep track of the maintenance on any line, be it a feeding tube, a drainage tube, a dialysis port, a catheter or an IV access point. Maintenance means cleaning the site every day. Maintenance means periodically changing the location of IV access points at some regular frequency. The four hospitals we were in disagreed on the frequency. However, none of them allowed usage of the same access point for more than five days.

Ask the hospital about their protocol and change-out frequency regarding IV line maintenance. Many nurses and doctors said to me that changing a line too frequently creates more risk of infection. While that makes sense to me on an intuitive level, I can tell you that over the course of eight-plus months, Bill never went septic within the 24-hour period following the introduction of a new line. He did, however, go septic from three, four and five-day-old line sites. Once I knew what the practice was at a particular hospital, I posted a sign over Bill's bed indicating when the next line change-out should occur.

Ensure that cleaning and inspection is performed on every line every day. Sometimes, if a site is starting to turn red, it is an indication of infection. If the offending line is removed promptly, you can often avoid problems. That is why a site inspection should be performed every day. If you can bear it, ask to watch when the nurse, doctor, or phlebotomist (specially trained blood worker) inspects/cleans/changes the line, then do a visual inspection yourself. If anything looks red, ask about it.

Sometimes when a patient is very sick and/or needs multiple IV lines, the anesthesiologist will install what is called a triple lumen. A triple lumen provides not one but three access points for intravenous solutions. Bill needed this type of access for many months due to the daily catastrophes he experienced.

One of the triple lumen access points was used for the introduction of liquid nutrition. Remember, not only was he unconscious for months, but in acute pancreatitis, the pancreas must rest to enable recovery. As a result, food intake must bypass the pancreas, either through the blood or through a feeding tube. When one of the triple lumen access points is used for a food supplement, the likelihood of line infection increases. So, be especially vigilant if your family member receives food through an IV.

One final comment about IV lines. A rehabilitation worker relayed the following story about her parents. Her father, a diabetic, was in the hospital and her mother was staying with him. One evening, a nurse brought a new IV solution into her father's room and began to hook the tubing up to her dad.

When her mother casually asked what the new drug was, the nurse informed her it was D10W, a sugar solution. What would have happened to her diabetic father had the sugar solution been administered and the question unasked? **Always** ask about what is being administered through IV lines!

Medications

Let's look at medications. We were in our twenty-second week in the hospital. I was sleeping on a cot at my husband's side. It was 1:15 am, and I woke up wondering if my husband had received one of his medications that night. Because the delivery system for this particular medication was experimental (a gel that crosses the skin/blood barrier), I was reasonably confident he had not received it because I would have seen the nurse apply it to his arm.

I approached the nurse and asked if Bill had received the medication that evening. She looked blank and said she did not even remember seeing it on the MARS (the sheet listing medications due for each patient). So I asked her to check. What a surprise! It was on the MARS and she had overlooked it. She had signed off that she had given it because it was supposed to have been included in a batch of other medications she went to the pharmacy to pick up.

Additionally, no internal alarms went off for her since she had never given this particular medicine in this way before. She apologized profusely and called the pharmacy.

Five minutes later, she was back in the room telling me there was a problem. No gel was made up, and the pharmacist on duty did not know how to mix it. Therefore, we could not give Bill his medication until the next day when someone who knew how to mix the gel could compound it.

The words I used in response to the pharmacist's answer are unprintable. Suffice it to say I did not accept his response. I asked the nurse to call back and ask the pharmacist three questions:

- Since when can the pharmacy service override the orders of the attending physicians?

- If this were a heart or blood pressure medication and a patient's life was at stake, would he still tell me we could not give Bill his medication? (In Bill's case, this medication was to relieve depression.)

- Why had he not suggested an alternative delivery system? (I knew there was one because we had used it before, in a pinch.)

Another surprise! The pharmacist called back ten minutes later stating he had found some of the gel. The nurse could come down and pick up the medication for immediate use. I took a tranquilizer and went to sleep. Another crisis averted, but at what cost? It is clear that had I not challenged the omission, Bill would not have received his medication that night.

The following morning, the primary doctor made rounds with his staff. When asked, "How did last night go?" I shared this story. One of his residents responded that the drug in question stays in the system for twenty-four hours, so we would have been OK, even if Bill had not received the drug. What's wrong with this answer?

Had this resident reviewed Bill's chart before her rounds, she would have known we were in the process of titrating (slowly building up) this drug to a therapeutic level following Bill's last episode in Intensive Care. Back in ICU, the doctors had ceased providing any drug that did not specifically address the problem that had brought him to Intensive Care. Although this happened without informing me, there is often good reason to withhold drugs that treat non-life threatening problems during a life-threatening crisis due to the possibility of an adverse drug reaction. (Since Bill's discharge, I have discovered that this particular drug is known to cause unpredictable drug-interaction responses.) This is a drug that is not supposed to be stopped suddenly. It was. This is also a drug whose effectiveness could be severely compromised if stopped and restarted. How did I know these facts? When the medication was stopped under similar circumstance in Hospital #2 and Bill's symptoms began to reappear, I talked to the pharmacy.

During the course of Bill's hospitalization, this medication was stopped and restarted four times. Guess who was responsible for identifying the stoppage and asking the doctors to restart it? His advocate—me.

We experienced the same problem with Bill's bedsore medication. Since his bedsore had become excruciatingly painful, Bill was receiving topical morphine to manage the pain. In the last three years, hospitals have begun to be much more aggressive in the area of pain management (see the *Pain Assessment Tool* in the Appendix).

While Bill was in the hospital, special training occurred around pain management in all four hospitals, and posters appeared proclaiming the patient's right to pain medication and how to measure pain levels. Nonetheless, without constant vigilance, his bedsore medicine was often overlooked. Is there a disparity between action and words?

Do not, I repeat, d**o not** allow any hospital worker to give your loved one **anything** without asking what it is and what it is for! If not caught, a mistake could quickly take your loved one from you. There is little emotional consolation in a malpractice lawsuit. Rosie O'Donnell once said, *"Speak and you are criticized. Be silent and you are damned."* Which would you rather be?

CHAPTER 11
Understand Every Procedure Used or Denied in Treatment

Security is a superstition. It does not exist in nature, nor do the children of men experience it. Avoiding danger is no safer in the long run than outright exposure. Life is either a daring adventure, or nothing. To keep our faces toward change and behave like free spirits in the presence of fate is strength undefeatable.

—Helen Keller, *Let Us Have Faith*

RECOMMENDATION #9: UNDERSTAND EVERY PROCEDURE USED OR DENIED IN TREATMENT.

Use the five "W's" to learn as much as you can from the doctors. Ask them:

- Who?
- What?

- **When?**
- **Where?**
- **Why?**

By now, the doctors and nurses should be used to (notice, I did not say, "comfortable with" or "like") your involvement in providing care for your loved one. You have done your homework (educated yourself in Chapter 9), and hopefully you are ready to move into a true partnership with the doctors and nurses.

Before we look at a process for becoming involved with procedures, I want to reiterate the most important procedure you and all the care providers can and should adopt—scrupulous hand washing! Dirty, non-sterile hands are a primary contributor to the spread of infection. You have a right and an obligation to protect your loved one by demanding (not requesting, demanding!) that doctors and nurses who treat your family member wash their hands upon entry and departure. Doctors making rounds can and do spread infection through failure to wash between rooms. This is so common there is a name for doctor-created disorders—iatrogenic disease. Interesting when in the Hippocratic oath doctors swear allegiance that begins with the words, "First, do no harm."

Understand Every Procedure

When I was young, I learned to memorize lists by associating letters with the title of the list. I have already associated the word Partnership with Procedures. I now want to give you an equation:

$$\text{WELLNESS} = \text{WE} \times \text{FIVE "W's"}$$

(Get the parallel? We = me, the patient and the healthcare providers, the Five W's = <u>W</u>ho, <u>W</u>hat, <u>W</u>hen, <u>W</u>here, <u>W</u>hy.)

Let's create a context. Any time a procedure is planned for your loved one, it suggests some change is anticipated, else why the procedure? We all experience the same process when dealing with change. We know it is much easier to keep people moving through the transition curve during change and to combat feelings of discouragement if they know:

- Where am I going?
- Why is this necessary?
- How will I get there?
- What part will everyone play in assuring I do get there?

This is where the Five W's and the "WE" in wellness come in. A well-thought-out procedure includes all of these elements and ensures your understanding and role in executing the decision-making procedure.

WELLNESS = WE x FIVE "W'S"

Before we begin defining the "W's," make certain that you are personally involved in every procedure that affects your loved one. This is not a case of doctor decides, patient complies. This is a case of "WE," a trinity, the doctor, the patient (if possible) and me (the advocate). If the doctor ignores any part of the "we," there is no trinity. What happens when you remove one of the legs of a tripod?

Ask the doctor all of the questions that follow…

- **Who:** Who *should* be involved in this procedure? Who *will* be involved in this procedure? Who will *not* be involved? Who will *play* each role? Who will actually *perform* the procedure? Who will keep you *informed* during the procedure? Who will *care* for your family member after the procedure?

    If you know who the players are and they all know the roles they will play, there is a far better chance of gaining their commitment and ensuring their readiness. Sometimes, due to staffing, illness and many other variables, the best possible medical partner is not

Understand Every Procedure

available on the day the procedure is scheduled. Does it make sense to delay the procedure? Is there greater risk in the delay or in the choice of a # 2 medical partner?

- **What:** What is *going* to happen? What *could* happen? What has the physician done to *prevent* the risk of complications? What other *alternatives* can be considered? What can you, the advocate, *do*, before, during and after the procedure? What will the *outcome* look like? What *will* it feel like for your loved one, the patient? What would the *physician do* if a member of his/her family was in the same position?

    The "what" of the discussion helps us know the road. It's like being given a map or a compass and told how to read it. Confidence in the outcome increases when we know the direction, where the detours exist and how long the trip will last.

- **When:** When *should* the procedure take place? When *will* the procedure take place? When can you expect to *see* your loved one *after* the procedure?

    The "when" of the procedure may be at risk due to hospital variables. What about *operating room* availability? What are the *consequences* of delay? Do they *offset* the benefits of waiting?

- **Where:** Where is the *best place* for this procedure to be performed? Where *will* the procedure be performed?

  The "where" of the procedure may also be at risk due to hospital variables. What about *equipment availability*? What are the *consequences* of delay? Do they *offset* the benefits of waiting?

- **Why:** Why are we *doing* this?

Bottom line, look for eye contact, cautiousness, candor and compassion from the physician. Ask yourself if you know what you can do as the advocate to improve the odds in favor of your loved one.

Now you have a framework for looking at any proposed procedure. Let's see what happens if you are denied your role as a partner in your loved one's care.

Upon admittance to Hospital #2, one of the doctors who chose not to partner with me denied Bill his needed kidney dialysis. Within twenty-four hours, Bill suffered his first case of sinus ventricular tachacardia (SVT), in which the heart races wildly out of control and requires cardioversion (electrical shock with the clappers on the chest). I believe this occurred because this doctor allowed the toxins to build up in Bill's body by denying him dialysis. Since I cannot prove this, the letter that follows will have to suffice.

I acknowledge the outrage contained in this correspondence and hope it will not interfere with your reading and understanding of the problems that occurred and my response to them. I cannot "quiet" my emotional language since this is a copy of the actual correspondence.

Incidentally, I am reasonably confident that even before September 11, 2001, I violated some federal laws in sending hazardous waste through the mail. If there are any postal workers reading this, please forgive me...

> *Copy of actual letter forwarded to offending physician. Names have been deleted to protect the guilty...*

Remember, as you read, a statement by Oliver Wendell Holmes – *"Beware how you take away hope from another human being."*

March 15, 2001

Dear Dr. X:

On the afternoon of December 11, 2000, my husband, William C. Buck (SS#XXX-XX-XXXX) was admitted to (your) hospital with Acute Pancreatitis, resulting in Multiple Organ Failure, including the kidneys.

On the evening of December 12, you came to his room and, without introducing yourself to me, asking any questions or examining my husband, you stated, "Although your husband has been dialyzed daily for some time, we will not be dialyzing him tonight." Understandably, I asked you why since, as a former resident of your state, I had been raised to believe that (your clinic) was the "be all, end all" of medical facilities in the world. After all, why else had I delivered him to you by air ambulance the preceding day?

Your response to me follows. "We have a female patient in the Emergency Room and unless we dialyze her, she will have to be intubated. Since your husband's kidneys have less than a 5 percent chance of restarting due to the length of time they have been shutdown, I have chosen to dialyze her over your husband."

You may or may not recall my response, which was, "Doctor, my husband has less than a 5 percent chance of being alive today. So, we are not going to talk statistics. This is a real human being laying in that bed and, if he needs to be dialyzed tonight, I expect you to find a way to dialyze him."

Enclosed please find a urine sample from this less than 5% former patient of yours. You see, I knew something that apparently you did not… His kidneys were going to do what his kidneys were going to do, with or without your inaccurate and heartlessly delivered prognosis.

I am pleased to report that he is alive today and will live a life without dialysis (following four and a-half months of kidney failure and your medical discharge of End Stage Renal Failure), no thanks to your statistics.

I am writing this letter on behalf of all the patients that will follow Bill Buck at (your clinic) or wherever you practice medicine. The next time you are tempted to quote statistics, remember Bill Buck.

Although I no longer believe that (your clinic) is the "be all, end all" of medical facilities in the world, I don't believe you know this.

> My experience with (your clinic) was that you all believed your publicity, and were consistently proved wrong in the case of my husband. The callous delivery of your triage assessment was inexcusable, even had you been right. You are human and cannot, with certainty OR statistics, predict who will regain kidney function. Remember that the next time you face a patient or family member and tell them about the function of a pair of kidneys.
>
> Sincerely yours,
>
> Jari Holland Buck
>
> Cc: Name, CEO
>
> Name, M.D., Chairman, Division of Nephrology

Now, how did I know what dialysis would do for Bill? I had pestered the nephrologist and dialysis nurse at the prior hospital to explain everything about the process and what it did. I also asked questions about what would happen if Bill was denied dialysis. In this case, refusal to consider me a care partner almost cost Bill his life. I would have had a hard time forgiving myself for not advocating harder had he died.

I am reasonably confident my letter and urine sample had little effect since, two weeks after sending it, I received the following reply from the treating physician.

> March 28, 2001
>
> Dear Mrs. Buck:
>
> Thank you very much for your letter dated March 15, 2001. I am extremely pleased to hear of your husband's progress. Please do not hesitate to contact me if you have any further questions.
>
> Sincerely,
>
> Dr. X

I received no response at all from the CEO of that facility although he was copied on my previous letter and received the following letter, as well. I even re-sent both these letters to the CEO when the same hospital tried to "solicit" us for a financial contribution in support of their not-for-profit arm. Still no response.

March 15, 2001

Dear Dr. BBB:

The purpose of this letter is to inform you of my extreme dissatisfaction with (your clinic) and the treatment provided to my husband. You will also note an additional enclosure to the Nephrologist who participated on my husband's team.

I was born and raised in (your state) and had always believed that (your clinic) was the premier medical facility in the world. No longer do I believe this. On the afternoon of December 11, 2000, my husband, William C. Buck (SS#XXX-XX-XXXX) was admitted to (your clinic) with Idiopathic Pancreatitis. The purpose of transferring him to (your clinic) was to determine if surgery was an appropriate intervention.

Having been in the hospital 24/7 with Bill since the onset of his Acute Pancreatitis (October 23, 2000) and given that he was intubated and kept heavily sedated, as his wife, I was responsible for making the health care decisions. Prior to admission at (your clinic), we had experienced the following:

- Respiratory failure
- Respirator plug which resulted in a Code
- Adult Respiratory Distress Syndrome
- Pneumonia
- Five septic events
- Shock liver
- Ileus
- Grand Mal seizures
- Acute renal failure
- Pseudocyst
- Suspected ruptured Pseudocyst
- Pancreatogenous ascites
- Depression
- Disseminated intravascular coagulation
- Rash and
- Anemia.

I am a trained Emergency Medical Technician and Masters Level Business consultant and made it a point to research, educate myself, ask questions and actively participate in the decision making process surrounding my husband's illness. That active process was denied me at (your clinic). Without going into excruciating detail, we experienced the following while at (your clinic):

- I was denied access to my husband's lab results for the first five days, in spite of frequent requests and reference to your Patient Rights brochure. On the 5th day, I contacted a Patient Rights advocate for the hospital and gave them the choice of providing the labs to me immediately or receiving a call from my attorney. According to this same Patient Rights advocate, it took him two and a-half hours to convince Dr. YYY, M.D. (the physician in charge) to provide the same to me.

- Bill was cardioverted on the evening of December 18, due to SVT's of 195 beats/minute. I was told this was common in ICU and subsequently, have been told otherwise.

- I have also been told that the most probable cause of SVT's in someone who was in the condition my husband was in is an imbalance in electrolytes. Since I was extremely knowledgeable about reading/understanding the labs, could it be that I was denied his labs because the treating physicians thought I might catch this?

- See the enclosed letter to Dr. XXX, D.O. regarding our experience with Nephrology.

- My husband transferred to (your clinic) off a Triadyne (rotating) bed. Since he had a tracheostomy and a Stage 1 breakdown on his coccyx, I did not expect (your clinic) to deny him a Triadyne bed, which (your clinic) did. How is it that during the time it took to transport him to (your clinic) from Kansas City that he improved sufficiently to deny him this bed? We continue to struggle with clearing a now Stage 2 breakdown, largely as a result of being denied the bed at (your clinic).

- Dr. YYY's team constantly attempted to get me to allow administration of Haldol for ICU Psychosis, which Bill did not have. I subsequently learned of a Haldol study being conducted at (your clinic). I wonder if that was not the reason for Dr. YYY's insistence?

- (Your clinic) made a decision to take my husband off Serazone for his bi-polar condition. No amount of discussion with Dr. YYY could get him to re-instate this drug. I asked for a psychiatric consult and when Dr. ZZZ, M.D. came to see me, she spent the majority of time with me and my mother-in-law asking us to discuss how we felt about my husband's illness and what we were doing to care for ourselves, not what she was invited or welcomed to do;

- I was "disciplined" by a nurse for allegedly reading my husbands file on the table outside his room. This was a result of a doctor seeing me from across the room with my head down over this file;

- One night, we experienced a ten minute delay in responding to an ICU nurse call button activation. I finally had to go stand outside Bill's room, gowned, gloved and masked due to MRSA, and yell for assistance;

- Pulmonary replaced his tracheostomy with a pediatric tracheostomy (Bill is 6'1", 185 pounds):

- The PIC line (your clinic) installed FELL OUT two days after it was placed;

- The GI team, headed by Dr, AAA, M.D. told us at least three times, and I quote, "If you cut him open, he will die." Could it be that (your clinic) was unwilling to risk its statistical recovery percentage because Bill was so high risk?

I am not interested in a "Sorry you had such a bad experience. We try hard," response to this letter. I did file a formal complaint with your Patient Right Advocacy team on the day of our departure.

The only type of response I would be interested in is a description of what (your clinic) is doing to address the above stated problems. Having now been in four different hospitals, I can state that in my experience, nowhere is the healthcare system more broken than at (your clinic). It is my opinion, and the opinion of both my mother and mother-in-law who were with me at (your clinic), that (your clinic) has totally forgotten the human component of healthcare.

I am grateful for one thing. When my husband finally had no other chance for survival but surgery, I was given two choices by our doctors – (your clinic) and (Hospital #4). Because of the experience we had previously had at (your clinic), I chose (Hospital #4). On January 13, they removed four basketball-sized pseudocysts form his abdomen and placed four Abramson pumps, seven pen rows and a passive T-tube. Thanks to the skill and courage of a fine surgeon at the (Hospital #4), Bill survived and will live a life with only one minor consequence (probable insulin dependency), no thanks to (your clinic's) prognosis. I have every confidence that, had I chosen (your clinic), the outcome would have been different and I would now be a widow. What a sad statement to make about a facility that I once believed to be the premier medical facility in the world ...

Sincerely yours,
Jari Holland Buck

If you ever wonder whether healthcare is truly broken, the procedures, treatment, and disinterest evinced by this world-renowned clinic should be sufficient to convince you. You must advocate for your family member. However, even if you do, as I did in this instance, you are not guaranteed success.

CHECKLIST F–Procedure Preparation

NUMBER	QUESTIONS FOR YOU TO ASK	√
1.	*Who:*	
a.	Who *should* be involved in this procedure?	
b.	Who *will* be involved in this procedure?	
c.	Who will *not* be involved?	
d.	Who will *play* each role?	
e.	Who will actually *perform* the procedure?	
f.	Who will keep you *informed* during the procedure?	
g.	Who will *care* for your family member after the procedure?	
2.	*What*:	
a.	What *is* going to happen?	
b.	What *could* happen?	
c.	What has the physician done to *prevent* the risk of complications?	
d.	What *can you*, the advocate, *do*, before, during and after the procedure?	

Understand Every Procedure

NUMBER	QUESTIONS FOR YOU TO ASK	√
e.	What other *alternatives* can be considered?	
f.	What will the *outcome* look like?	
g.	What is it going to *feel* like for your loved one, the patient?	
h.	What would the *physician* do if a member of his/her own family was in the same position?	
3.	*When:*	
a.	When *should* the procedure take place?	
b.	When *will* the procedure take place?	
c.	When can I *expect* to see my loved one after the procedure?	
4.	*Where:*	
a.	Where is the *best place* for this procedure to be performed?	
b.	Where will the procedure take place?	
5.	*Why:*	
a.	*Why* are we doing this?	

CHAPTER 12
Keep Track of All Supplies and Other Duplicated or Unwarranted Services Used in Treatment

No one is hurt by doing the right thing.
—Hawaiian Proverb, Feldman, *A World Treasury*

Learn the rules so you know how to break them properly.
—Nepalese Good Luck Mantra

It is better to prevent than cure.
—Peruvian Proverb, Feldman, *A World Treasury*

RECOMMENDATION #10: KEEP TRACK OF ALL SUPPLIES AND OTHER DUPLICATED OR UNWARRANTED SERVICES USED IN TREATMENT.

Refuse to pay for duplicate or unnecessary supplies and services. As you accumulate supplies, post signs in the hospital room for staff to look in specified drawers/places for usable supplies.

When Bill left the hospital, he had fourteen blood pressure cuffs and three pairs of $600 inflatable boots designed to prevent blood clots. The other supply duplications were equally excessive. These duplications occurred primarily because the nurse failed to check for the existence of the supply before entering the room with it in hand. And, because Bill had MRSA (contagious staph infection), once it was in the room, we owned it!

No amount of signs posted by me **(Please do not order or provide new supplies to this room without first checking the bedside nightstand!** was taped to the wall over his head *and* on the door upon entry) stopped the inflow of supplies.

Part of your 24/7 duty lies in informing the hospital staff of what you will not pay for as a result of them ignoring your signs. Not only must you inform them, but also you must insist on *seeing* the charge actually removed from the record.

This is the point where nurses sometimes get a bit testy. I frequently had a nurse say she would remove a charge only to have it show up on the hospital bill. Once it gets there, it is

Keep Track of All Supplies and Services

virtually impossible to get it removed, so you must act upstream from this event.

This also includes acting on doctor consultations that were not requested and are not warranted. For example, because I was present in Bill's room 24/7, I was there when a plastic surgeon appeared to **ass**ess (pun intended) Bill for the need for plastic surgery. Guess what part of the body he inspected? His butt! Yes, a plastic surgeon assessed the need for plastic surgery at the site of Bill's bedsore! That part of the body hardly merited a "cosmetic" treatment! I contested the need for this consult, the doctor agreed and we managed to get it removed from the bill.

Yes, this is dumb. Yes, this should not happen, but it does! Just remember for every duplicate or unnecessary dollar you get taken off the bill, that amount of money remains on the lifetime maximum of your health insurance policy for what it is intended to provide—healthcare.

CHAPTER 13
Stay in the Room 24/7

The greatest gift you can give another is the purity of your attention.

—Richard Moss, *The I That is We*

RECOMMENDATION #11: STAY IN THE ROOM 24/7. This means twenty-four hours a day seven days a week. You are the guardian. Maintain your post or pass it to someone else. This is especially true in Intensive Care. AWOL could mean DEAD.

I have tried in every way I know to demonstrate that the job of advocacy we have chosen for ourselves is a full-time job. I am not asking you personally to be there 24/7, but simply that some combination of educated advocates be there 24/7.

There are certain times when it is absolutely critical you be present with your loved one, unless you are guaranteed he/she will be constantly monitored by someone else in the room. Such times include when your family member is eating, bathing, exercising, being transferred or experiencing a procedure such as an x-ray. Too many things can go wrong.

If you are the primary advocate, as I was, I'm sure you have feelings and opinions about that. I shut down my consulting practice to be at Bill's side day and night. Had I lost clients I didn't want to lose, I'm sure I would have been disappointed and possibly angry. Luckily, that didn't happen for me, but some comparable loss may affect you. Had we not had great health insurance, we would have had no choice but to declare bankruptcy as a result of astronomical medical bills. That didn't happen for us, but some comparable financial loss may affect you. Had both of us not had disability insurance, we would have suffered, at a minimum, extreme financial hardship. That didn't happen for us, but some financial loss may affect you.

The second most important loss we did not experience was the loss of friends and family. Without exception, all stood with us and helped us through the most difficult time of our lives. They continue to offer support to this day.

The most important loss we have *not* suffered is the loss of each other. I believe my vigil played a critical role in preventing that loss. If I have yet to convince you of this, I offer this story.

WHISPERS

A young and very successful executive was traveling down a neighborhood street. He was going a bit too fast in his new Jaguar. He was watching for kids darting out from between parked cars and slowed down when he thought he saw something. As his car passed, no children appeared. Instead, a brick smashed into the Jag's side door! He slammed on the brakes, spun the Jag back to the spot from where the brick had been thrown. He jumped out of the car, grabbed some kid and pushed him up against a parked car, shouting, "What was that all about and who are you? Just what the heck are you doing?"

Building up a head of steam, he went on. "That's a new car and that brick you threw is gonna cost you a lot of money. Why did you do it?"

"Please, mister, please, I'm sorry! I didn't know what else to do!" pleaded the youngster. "I threw the brick because no one else would stop."

Tears were dripping down the boy's chin as he pointed around the parked car. "It's my brother," he said. "He rolled off the curb and fell out of his wheelchair and I can't lift him up." Sobbing, the boy asked the executive, "Would you please help me get him back into his wheelchair? He's hurt and he's too heavy for me."

24/7 or Dead

Moved beyond words, the driver tried desperately to swallow the rapidly swelling lump in his throat. Straining, he lifted the young man back into the wheelchair and took out his handkerchief and wiped the scrapes and cuts, checking to see that everything was going to be okay. "Thank you, sir! God bless you!"

He then watched the boy push his brother down the sidewalk toward their home. It was a long walk back to his Jaguar, a long and slow walk. He never did repair the side door. He kept the dent to remind him not to go through life so fast that someone has to throw a brick at you to get your attention.

Life whispers in your soul and speaks to your heart. Sometimes, when you don't have the time to listen, life throws a brick at your head. It's your choice: Listen to the whispers of your soul or wait for the brick.

This is a brick! Stay in that room 24/7 or risk losing the battle through your lack of vigilance. With your vigilance comes the certainty you will never have to second-guess yourself about whether you did everything you could, **because you did!**

CHAPTER 14
Pray

Believe more deeply. Hold your face up to the light, even though for the moment you do not see.

—Bill Wilson, Co-Founder of Alcoholics Anonymous

RECOMMENDATION #12: PRAY.

Let me be clear. I strongly believe in the power of prayer, whether it is your prayer or the prayer of others. In fact, documented studies show patients who are prayed for have a greater probability of survival. Although the "why" of these results cannot be explained, the results speak for themselves.

In our case, people all over the world were praying for Bill. And, most touchingly, the church across the street from our house put Bill into their prayer circle. One of Bill's coworkers, who attended this church, asked the congregation to pray on

Bill's behalf. Every week, Mildred, who headed up the prayer circle, would call for an update on Bill's condition. Both she and other friends would ask, "What body part should we pray for this week?"

There was a direct correlation between the body part offered up in prayer and the sequence of body part recoveries Bill experienced. Specifically, Bill's kidneys came back on line after weeks of prayer focus. Later, his feeding tube came out and he began to eat following a similar focus. Gratitude came in big gulps of air for me and of food for Bill.

How we pray and to whom is our personal choice. Embrace your own belief system and practice what it tells you.

Spirituality, unlike religion, is a private matter, a search for personal identity and meaning in life. Unlike religion, it does not require a particular place for its exercise, nor does it require a priesthood. Its temple is the mind of the individual, and its altar is the state of consciousness that comes about through deep meditation and prayer.

—Ervin Laszlo

If you need to know more about your faith, contact your

- minister
- rabbi
- priest
- teacher
- imam
- reverend
- elder
- shaman
- holy man/woman
- church leader

Be very clear about what you want, and do not hesitate to ask for it in prayer. You have nothing to lose and everything to gain. So does your loved one, even if the answer is "No." You will know then that you have done everything that could be done and you can let go and surrender.

CHAPTER 15
Surrender

Have patience with everything unresolved in your heart
and try to love the questions themselves ...
Don't search for the answers,
which could not be given to you now,
because you would not be able to live them.
And the point is, to live everything.
Live the questions now.
Perhaps then, someday far in the future,
you will gradually, without even noticing it,
live your way into the answer.

—Rainer Maria Rilke

RECOMMENDATION #13: SURRENDER.
There is nothing like a serious illness to remind us how powerless we are. In Alcoholics Anonymous, the First Step reads, "Made a decision to turn my will and my life over to the care of God, as I understood Him." This is

surrender. You are responsible for the input. You are not responsible for the outcome.

According to Rick Work in his book, *Awaken to the Healer Within*, certain universal laws govern all creation. In Chapter 8, we looked at two of them, the **Law of Magnetic Attraction** and the **Law of Creative Manifestation.** Here is third.

Reprinted with permission

The Law of Allowing

This is the most difficult law of all. Put your thoughts into universal consciousness, reinforced by desire. Then step aside and allow the universe to manifest it for you. If you are hoping, then you are not allowing. If you have expectations, you are not allowing.

If you have expectations, it is like saying, "Okay, God, this is what I want. Now, let me tell you how to do it!" And God responds by saying, "For heaven's sake, get out of the way and let me do it for you." The more you expect, the more you hope, the more you try to manage or control, the more you will interfere and retard the manifesting of your desires. The Law of Allowing means just that. After all, the Master said, "Ask and ye shall receive." He didn't say, "Ask and we'll go have a committee meeting and take a vote on it."

Surrender

If you have done everything discussed in the previous chapters, you have done everything you can. It is time to surrender, to let go. Sometimes we need help understanding how and when to surrender. The most helpful guidance I have ever found is in a book published by C. D. Scott and D. T. Jaffe entitled *Making Personal Changes*. It provides a grid that helps us determine an appropriate response to a given situation.

PERSONAL POWER—GETTING WHAT YOU WANT

	CAN CONTROL	*CAN'T CONTROL*
TAKE ACTION	**MASTERY** achievement & success	**CEASELESS STRIVING** frustration & anger
NO ACTION	**GIVING UP** helpless & hopeless	**LETTING GO** relief & release

Here's what this means. In life, there are some things you *can* control and some things you *cannot* control. Recognizing that there are some things you *cannot* control will help you understand whether you should be trying to take action.

When you *can* control something, such as how you act, treat healthcare providers, respond to crises, and learn new medical information, you should take action. **Do it! Learn it! Work at it! Master it!** According to Scott and Jaffee, this will give you feelings of achievement and success. For example, I learned everything I could about Bill's disease, treatment, medications, procedures, and prognosis, and was successful in many of my efforts.

On the other hand, if you *can't* control something, don't keep trying. If you keep trying, **ceaselessly striving** to do something that is out of your control, you end up frustrated and angry. In fact, you can test the difference between what you *can* and *cannot* control that way. If you are feeling frustrated and angry, you are probably trying to do something about something that is out of your control. For example, I got frustrated and angry when I **ceaselessly strove** to make the doctors at Hospital #2 do what I wanted them to do.

When I finally complained to the Patient Rights representative, I moved back into **mastery**, and then into **letting go**.

If you *can't* control it, like you can't control whether your loved one lives or dies, **let go**, find the relief and release of admitting it is out of your control and put your energies elsewhere—such as into mastering what you can control.

But if you *can* control it, don't fail to take action. That would be **giving up.** If you are feeling helpless and hopeless, that's a good indicator you have given up when you could be doing something for your loved one or yourself. You want to be in **mastery** and in **letting go**. Over nearly nine months, only Hospital #2 gave up on Bill.

If you add your voice to **mastery**, by the Native American definition of leadership, you cannot be ignored. According to the Native Americans, true leaders (advocates) have three kinds of power:

- **presence** = charisma
- **communication skills**
- **position** = a committed opinion about a subject

The presence of all three indicates "big personal power" and you cannot be ignored!

Unfortunately, sometimes letting go is an active process because, in order to make a decision of that magnitude, you will have to set aside your own desire to keep your loved one with you. At some point, you and your healthcare partners may come to the conclusion that the quality of life remaining for your loved one is poor. If a DNR (Do Not Resuscitate) is in place, it may be that your loved one will pass peacefully on their own. In the absence of such direction, you may be left with an excruciating decision —what medical intervention will I allow in maintaining the life of my loved one? This is a very personal decision and one that must be made with great care and compassion. It is often helpful to involve other physicians or non-physician mediators, such as the hospital ethicists, patient advocates, social workers and clergy members, in the decision-making process. Once values are explicitly discussed and differences clarified, a plan may be agreed upon by which all parties can abide.

By now, the healthcare providers cannot ignore you! Feel good about what you have done for your loved one and keep on doing. But remember, we cannot control life and death—our own or another's. There is a higher order of things at work in the universe.

Approach each day *As If You Knew* (a poem circulated on the Internet in tribute to those lost on September 11, 2001).

Surrender

If I knew it would be the last time I'd see you fall asleep,
I would tuck you in more tightly and pray the Lord your soul to keep.

If I knew it would be the last time I'd see you walk out the door,
I would give you a hug and kiss and call you back for one more.

If I knew it would be the last time I'd hear your voice lifted up in praise,
I would videotape each action and word, so I could play them back day after day.

If I knew it would be the last time, I could spare an extra minute to
Stop and say "I love you," instead of assuming you would KNOW I do.

If I knew it would be the last time I would be there to share your day,
Well, I'm sure you'll have so many more, so I can let just this one slip away.

For surely there's always tomorrow to make up for an oversight, and
We always get a second chance to make everything just right.

There will always be another day to say "I love you,"
And certainly there's another chance to say our "Anything I can do?"

But just in case I might be wrong, and today is all I get,
I'd like to say how much I love you and I hope we never forget.

24/7 or Dead

Tomorrow is not promised to anyone, young or old alike,
And today may be the last chance you get to hold your loved one tight.

So if you're waiting for tomorrow, why not do it today?
For if tomorrow never comes, you'll surely regret the day,

That you didn't take extra time for a smile, a hug, or a kiss and
You were too busy to grant someone what turned out to be their one last wish.

So hold your loved ones close today, and whisper in their ear,
Tell them how much you love them and you'll always hold them dear.

Take time to say, "I'm sorry," "Please forgive me," "Thank you," or "It's okay".
And if tomorrow never comes, you'll have no regrets about today.

CHAPTER 16
Take Care of Yourself

Help us to be the always hopeful gardeners of the spirit who know without darkness
nothing comes to birth. As without light nothing flowers.

—May Sarton, *Journal of a Solitude*

RECOMMENDATION #14: TAKE CARE OF YOURSELF.

You are of no value to your loved one if you go down for the count. Sacrificing your own health for another is not what anyone who loves us would want us to do.

Take care of yourself is my first and last recommendation because all other recommendations depend on it.

The Alzheimer's Association has identified ten warning signs of caregiver stress, and has generously granted permission to reprint them here. I offer them now as the final warning, a warning designed to prevent needing an advocate for yourself, because **you** end up in the hospital!

Reprinted with permission by the Alzheimer's Association, 1995

TEN WARNING SIGNS OF CAREGIVER STRESS

1. **DENIAL about the disease and its effects on the person who has been diagnosed**. Denial in our case could make us believe that the hospital will care for our loved ones with the same attention and love that we ourselves can provide.

2. **ANGER at the person who is sick or others. Anger about the treatments. Anger that people don't understand what is going on**. In my case, I never got angry at Bill. I did, however, get very angry at the hospital staff on occasion and my anger did not help resolve the issues.

3. **SOCIAL WITHDRAWAL from friends and activities that once brought pleasure**. I was so very tired at the hospital that if my friends had not come to me, I would not have asked them to do so. The same thing has happened during Bill's recovery at home. And yet, it is these very people and the cherished activities of my free time that refresh and revitalize me.

Take Care of Yourself

4. **ANXIETY about facing another day and what the future holds**. I did get weary of constant vigilance. I often wondered if anything else could go wrong! Sometimes, I still do…

5. **DEPRESSION begins to break your spirit and affects your ability to cope**. Watch out for this sneaky feeling! It creeps up on you and gets you in its grasp with little to no warning. And, because it is so gradual, it is often hard to identify and, for some of us (like me), hard to own.

6. **EXHAUSTION makes it nearly impossible to complete necessary daily tasks**. We frequently hear the term "double digit inflation" from our politicians. Well, I can beat that! I have quintuple digit sleep loss!

7. **SLEEPLESSNESS caused by a never-ending list of concerns**. Talk about lists! In the hospital, there were lists of compromised body parts, lists of medication interactions to watch for, lists of supplies, lists of nurse's names, lists of doctor's names and on and on and on! You are only one person, even if you are super human!

8. **IRRITABILITY leads to moodiness and triggers negative responses and reactions**. It is only fair to you and all the care givers that helped Bill (and I) survive to admit that, on RARE occasions, I MAY have overreacted just a tiny bit. Glad I don't have to get consensus on that statement!

9. **LACK OF CONCENTRATION makes it difficult to perform familiar tasks**. Even after eight and a-half months in the hospital, I would sometimes find myself

walking down the hall to the nurse's station and not able to recall the purpose of my trip.

10. **HEALTH PROBLEMS begin to take their toll, both mentally and physically**. Shortly after Bill arrived home, I ended up at the foot doctor with excruciating heel pain because of all the walking I had done at the hospital and was still doing at home. I also found myself in therapy, learning how to deal with **my** personal losses as well as the "new man" in **my** life, Bill.

Neither you or your loved one can go through a life-changing event like Bill and I did without having your life change. Bill is in therapy to deal with his personal losses as well as the "new woman" in his life, me. Because we are different, because we have both experienced loss, and because we discovered that life cannot be controlled, we are slowly learning that life can only be lived. This continues to be a hard lesson.

Assuming you have been taking care of yourself throughout this process, hope is the last piece of the puzzle. As so eloquently stated by Emily Dickinson, *"Hope is the thing with feathers that perches in the soul and sings the tune without the words and never stops at all."*

No matter what the outcome is, time will help. We had to wait three months for Bill's pseudocysts to "ripen." We had to wait five months following surgery for Bill's discharge. Bill continues to wait for an explanation of what he is to do with the rest of his life. I had to wait six months before the pain of what we had gone through was no longer so potent and debilitating that I could write this book.

And, no matter what the outcome is, whatever you did was the best you could do, and the rest is out of our hands. Spending time "shoulding" on yourself does not help recovery. It only prolongs it. Be gentle, love yourself, and trust this process. Know that even as a stranger, I am very proud that you did what you could. I am also grateful if I played some small role in assisting you.

We started this journey together with a reminder that we do this for love. And we did. May you walk hand in hand with your loved one through all of eternity.

Once upon a time there was an island where all the feelings lived: Happiness, Sadness, Knowledge, and all the others, including Love.

One day it was announced to all of the feelings that the island was going to sink to the bottom of the ocean. So all the feelings prepared their boats to leave.

Love was the only one that stayed. She wanted to preserve the island paradise until the last possible moment.

24/7 or Dead

When the island was almost totally under, Love decided it was time to leave. She began looking for someone to ask for help.

Just then Richness was passing by in a grand boat. Love asked, "Richness, can I come with you on your boat?"

Richness answered, "I'm sorry, but there is a lot of silver and gold on my boat, and there would be no room for you anywhere."

Then Love decided to ask Vanity for help, who was passing in a beautiful vessel. Love cried out, "Vanity, help me please."

"I can't help you," Vanity said. " You are all wet and will damage my beautiful boat."

Next, Love saw Sadness passing by. Love said, "Sadness, please let me go with you." Sadness answered, "Love, I'm sorry, but I just need to be alone now."

Then Love saw Happiness. Love cried out, "Happiness, please take me with you." But Happiness was so overjoyed that he didn't hear Love calling to him.

Love began to cry. Then she heard a voice say, "Come Love, I will take you with me." It was an elder.

Love felt so blessed and overjoyed that she forgot to ask the elder his name.

When they arrived on land, the elder went on his way. Love realized how much she owed the elder.

Love then found Knowledge and asked, "Who was it that helped me?"

"It was Time," Knowledge answered.

"But why did Time help me when no one else would?" Love asked.

Knowledge smiled, and with deep wisdom and sincerity, answered, "Because only Time is capable of understanding how great Love is."

APPENDIX

Reprinted with permission from the National Patient Safety Foundation, 2003
515 North State Street,
Chicago, IL 60610, (312) 464-4848, http://www.npsf.org,
©2003.

NATIONAL PATIENT SAFETY FOUNDATION® (NPSF)

A Consumer Fact Sheet: The Role of the Patient Advocate

Illness is a stressful time for patients as well as for their families. The best laid plans can go awry, judgment is impaired, and put simply, you are not at your best when you are sick. Patients need someone who can look out for their best interests and help navigate the confusing healthcare system–in other words, an advocate.

What is a Patient Advocate? An advocate is a "supporter, believer, sponsor, promoter, campaigner, backer, or spokesperson." It is important to consider all of these aspects when choosing an advocate for yourself or someone in your family. An effective advocate is someone you trust who is willing to act on your behalf as well as someone who can work well with other members of your healthcare team such as your doctors and nurses.

An advocate may be a member of your family, such as a spouse, a child, another family member, or a close friend. Another type of advocate is a professional advocate. Hospitals usually have professionals who play this role called Patient Representatives or Patient Advocates. Social workers, nurses and chaplains may also fill this role. These advocates can often be very helpful in cutting through red tape. It is helpful to find out if your hospital has professional advocates available, and how they may be able to help you.

Using an advocate–getting started

1. Select a person you can communicate with and you trust. It's important to pick someone who is assertive and who has good communication skills. Make sure the person you select is willing and able to be the type of advocate you need.

2. Decide what you want help with and what you want to handle on your own. For example, you may want help with:

    a. clarifying your options for hospitals, doctors, diagnostic tests and procedures or treatment choices

    b. getting information or asking specific questions

c. writing down information you receive from your caregivers, as well as any questions you may have

d. assuring your wishes are carried out when you may not be able to do that by yourself.

3. Decide if you would like your advocate to accompany you to tests, appointments, treatments and procedures. If so, insist your doctor and other caregivers allow this.

4. Be very clear with your advocate about what you would like them to know and be involved in:

   a. treatment decisions?

   b. any change in your condition?

   c. test results?

   d. keeping track of medications?

5. Let your physician and those caring for you know who your advocate is and how you want them involved in your care.

6. Arrange for your designated advocate to be the spokesperson for the rest of your family and make sure your other family members know this. This will provide a consistent communication link for your caregivers and

can help to minimize confusion and misunderstandings within your family. Make sure your doctor and nurses have your advocate's phone number and make sure your advocate has the numbers for your providers, hospital and pharmacy, as well as anyone else you may want to contact in the case of an emergency.

Patient safety suggestions–getting started

1. Ask questions, read labels, ask for explanations; take nothing for granted.

2. Ask for written information about medications you are given in the hospital and when you go home.

3. Don't be afraid to question something you don't understand.

4. Insist that staff check your armband before they take you for tests, give you oral medications or put anything in your intravenous fluids.

5. Pay attention to your symptoms–pain, nausea, drowsiness, dizziness. Often these are side effects of medications or treatments. Don't ignore them. Make sure your doctors and nurses know how you are feeling.

6. Always ask for help if something just doesn't "feel right".

7. Ask what, when, why and how about everything.

Reprinted with permission from the Gary Barg, author of *The Fearless Caregiver, How to Get the Best Care for Your Loved One and Still Have a Life of Your Own* and Editor-in-Chief and Publisher of *caregiver.com*

The Fearless Caregiver Manifesto

How to Get the Best Care for Your Loved One and Still Have a Life of Your Own

I will fearlessly assess my personal strengths and weaknesses, work diligently to bolster my weaknesses and to graciously recognize my strengths.

I will fearlessly make my voice be heard with regard to my loved ones care and be a strong ally to those professional caregivers committed to caring for my loved one and a fearless shield against those not committed to caring for my loved one.

I will fearlessly not sign or approve anything I do not understand, and will steadfastly request the information I need until I am satisfied with the explanations.

I will fearlessly ensure that all of the necessary documents are in place in order for my wishes and my loved ones wishes to be met in case of a medical emergency. These will include Durable Medical Powers of Attorney, Wills, Trusts and Living Wills.

I will fearlessly learn all I can about my loved one's healthcare needs and become an integral member of his or her medical care team.

I will fearlessly seek out other caregivers or care organizations and join an appropriate support group; I realize that there is strength in numbers and will not isolate myself from those who are also caring for their loved ones.

I will fearlessly care for my physical and emotional health as well as I care for my loved one's, I will recognize the signs of my own exhaustion and depression, and I will allow myself to take respite breaks and to care for myself on a regular basis.

I will fearlessly develop a personal support system of friends and family and remember that others also love my loved one and are willing to help if I let them know what they can do to support my caregiving.

I will fearlessly honor my loved one's wishes, as I know them to be, unless these wishes endanger their health or mine.

I will fearlessly acknowledge when providing appropriate care for my loved one becomes impossible either because of his or her condition or my own and seek other solutions for my loved one's caregiving needs.

Pain Assessment Tool

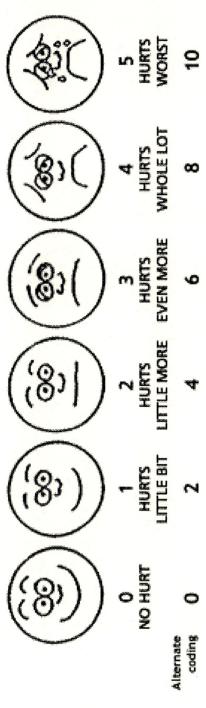

Sample Durable Power of Attorney – Healthcare

EXAMPLE ONLY. DO NOT COPY.
Each state has different requirements.
Consult with a legal advisor for access to documents appropriate for your state.

State of

County of

This Power of Attorney is made on (date)_____

I, (name) _____, of (street address) _____,
(city) _____, (county) _____, (state) _____

(zip)_____, appoint (spouse or other party) _____,

of (street address) _____, (city) _____,

(county) _____, (state) _____

(zip)_____, as my attorney-in-fact to act for me, and in my name in any way I could act in person, to make any and all decisions for me concerning my personal care, medical treatment, hospitalization and healthcare in accordance with the terms of this Durable Power of Attorney.

Attorney-in-fact is granted authority to require, withhold or withdraw any type of medical treatment or procedure, in accordance with the terms of this Durable Power of Attorney, even though my death may ensue. Attorney-in-fact shall have the same access to my judicial records that I would have if I were in full health, including the right to disclose the contents to others. Attorney-in-fact shall also have full power to make a disposition of any part or all of my body for medical purposes, to authorize an autopsy and to direct the disposition of my remains.

The above grant of power is intended to be a broad as possible so that attorney-in-fact will have authority to make any decision I could make to obtain or terminate any type of healthcare, including withdrawal of food and water and other life-sustaining measures if attorney-in-fact believes such action would be consistent with my intent and desires.

This Power of Attorney shall become effective on [date]. This Power of Attorney shall terminate upon a written revocation by [name] or by a court of competent jurisdiction.

If any attorney-in-fact named by me shall die, become legally disabled, resign, refuse to act or be unavailable, I name the following persons, each to act alone and successively in the order named, as successors to attorney-in-fact: (different party than above), (street address) _____,

(city) _____, (county) _____, (state) ____ (zip) _____,

If a guardian of my person is to be appointed, I nominate the following person to serve as guardian: (spouse or other party), of address) _____, (city) _____

(county) _____, (state) _____ (zip) .

I am fully informed as to all of the contents of this form and understand the full import of this grant of powers to my attorney-in-fact.

_____   _____
        (name)   (date)

Sample Living Will

EXAMPLE ONLY. DO NOT COPY.

Each state has different requirements. Consult with a legal advisor for access to documents appropriate for your state.

DECLARATION IN CONFORMANCE WITH (state) STATUTES (number/s)

I have the primary right to make my own decisions concerning treatment that might unduly prolong the dying process. By this declaration I express to my physician, family and friends my intent. If I should have a terminal condition, it is my desire my dying not be prolonged by administration of death-prolonging procedures. If my condition is terminal and I am unable to participate in decisions regarding my medical treatment, I direct that my attending physician to withhold or withdraw medical procedures that merely prolong the dying process and are not necessary to my comfort or to alleviate pain. It is not my intent to authorize affirmative or deliberate acts or omissions to shorten my life rather only to permit the natural process of dying.

_____ _____
(name)   (date)

City of residence: _____
County of residence: _____

State of residence: _____

The declarant is known to me, is eighteen years of age or older, of sound mind and voluntarily signed this document in my presence.

Witness_____

Address:_____

Witness_____

Address:_____

Sample Power of Attorney

EXAMPLE ONLY. DO NOT COPY.
Each state has different requirements.
Consult with a legal advisor for access to documents appropriate for your state.

KNOW ALL MEN BY THESE PRESENTS:

(name) _____, hereinafter referred to as PRINCIPAL, in the County of _____, State of ____ _____ does appoint (name) _____ his true and lawful attorney.

In principal's name, and for principal's use and benefit, said attorney is authorized hereby;

(1) To demand, sue for, collect, and receive all money, debts, accounts, legacies, bequests, interest, dividends, annuities, and demands as are now or shall hereafter become due, payable, or belonging to principal, and take all lawful means, for the recovery thereof and to compromise the same and give discharges for the same;

(2) To buy and sell land, make contracts of every kind relative to land, any interest therein or the possession thereof, and to take possession and exercise control over the use thereof;

(3) To lease, buy, sell, mortgage, hypothecate, assign, transfer, and in any manner deal with goods, wares and merchandise, chooses in action, certificates or shares of capital stock, and

other property in possession or in action, and to make, do, and transact all and every kind of business of whatever nature;

(4) To execute, acknowledge, and deliver contracts of sale, escrow instructions, deeds, leases including leases for minerals and hydrocarbon substances and assignments of leases, covenants, agreements and assignments of agreements, mortgages and assignments of mortgages, conveyances in trust, to secure indebtedness or other obligations, and assign the beneficial interest thereunder, subordinations of liens or encumbrances, bills of lading, receipts, evidences of debt, releases, bonds, notes, bills, requests to reconvey deeds of trust, partial or full judgments, satisfactions of mortgages, and other debts, and other written instruments of whatever kind and nature, all upon such terms and conditions as said attorney shall approve.

Giving and granting to said attorney full power and authority to do all and every act and thing whatsoever requisite and necessary to be done relative to any of the foregoing as fully to all intents and purposes as principal might or could do if personally present.

All that said attorney shall lawfully do or cause to be done under the authority of this Power of Attorney is expressly approved.

_____   _____
          (name)   (date)

Reprinted with permission by the author

Sample Patient Rights Statement

EXAMPLE ONLY.
Each hospital has its own personalized Patient Rights Statement.
Consult your hospital.

PATIENT RIGHTS

Quality patient care is the primary concern of [Sample Hospital]'s Heath System. You or your designated representative, have the right to:

- Treatment without discrimination as to race, age, religion, sex, national origin, disability, or source of payment.
- Considerate and respectful care.
- Receive care in a safe setting free from abuse, harassment and neglect.
- Be free from restraints or seclusion, imposed as a means of coercion, discipline, convenience or retaliation by staff.
- Understandable information concerning diagnosis, treatment and prognosis, and financial implications of treatment choices.

- The identity of those involved in your care.
- Involvement in medical decision-making including refusal of care and treatment, to the extent permitted by law, and to be informed of the medical consequences of refusal.
- Make decisions through advanced directives such a Living Will, healthcare proxy, or Durable Medical Power of Attorney.
- Appoint a surrogate to make healthcare decisions on your behalf to the extent permitted by law.
- Sensitivity addressing issues related to care at the end of life.
- Privacy.
- Confidentiality of information.
- Reasonable access to review the medical records, pertaining to your care, and to receive copies of these records for a reasonable photocopying fee.
- Receive medically appropriate care.
- Knowledge related to business relationships of the provider that might affect care.
- Decline participation in experimental treatments.
- Be informed of hospital policies and resources, such as Patient Advocates and the ethics committee.
- Access an internal grievance process and appeal to an external agency.

- Expect a family member (or representative) and your physician will be notified of your admission to the hospital, unless you request otherwise.
- Be informed of your rights in writing.
- Unrestricted access to communication, visitors, mail and telephone calls, unless clinically contraindicated. Any restrictions must be fully explained to the patient.
- The appropriate assessment and management of pain.
- Have your rights protected during research, investigation and clinical trials involving human subjects.
- Access pastoral care and spiritual services.
- Protective oversight while you are in the hospital.
- Be informed of and participate in treatment decisions and the care planning process.
- Participate in discharge planning, including being informed of service options that are available and choice of agencies.
- Have personal possessions brought to the hospital reasonably protected.
- Expect a reasonable response to your need/request for assistance in effective communication, regardless of language or disability.

We at [Sample Hospital] welcome your input concerning the care and treatment provided to you. Information received regarding compliments and concerns are tracked and trended in a confidential computer system. This information assists us in our continuing goal of improving care for you and other future patients and customers.

PATIENT COMPLIMENTS

Our primary goal at [Sample Hospital] is to make your stay as pleasant as possible. Compliments are welcome and will be shared with the [Sample Hospital] staff involved.

PATIENT CONCERNS

Most patient concerns can be handled by [Sample Hospital] associates at the time the concern is raised. [Sample Hospital] associates are encouraged to resolve concerns to the best of their ability with the resources at hand.

In addition, the Patient Advocate Department serves as a liaison between patients, their families, and the hospital. The Patient Advocate transcends departmental lines and interacts with staff at all levels within the organization.

To reach the Patient Advocate while you are in the hospital please call ext. XXXX, or (outside direct dial number) from outside the hospital. The Patient Advocate is available between the hours of 7:00 a.m.–4:30 p.m. Monday through Friday.

After hours, weekends, and holidays, assistance may be obtained by calling the hospital operator at "0" while in the hospital or (the outside general hospital number) from outside the hospital.

Once your concern is received, we will start investigating the matter within 24 hours.

NOTICE OF PATIENT GRIEVANCE PROCEDURE

A patient grievance is a formal written or verbal grievance that is filed by a patient, when a patient issue cannot be resolved promptly by staff present. Exercising your right to the grievance process will not compromise patient care. Confidentiality will be respected at all times. The expectation is that the facility will handle relatively minor changes in a timely manner with the need for a written facility response.

You have the right to lodge a grievance with any State agency directly, regardless of whether you have first used the hospital's grievance procedure. A list of state advocacy agencies and phone numbers is provided on the back of this brochure.

PATIENT RESPONSIBILITIES

As a patient, you, your family or your designated representatives have the responsibility to:

- Provide information: to the best of your knowledge, accurate and complete information about present complaints, past illnesses, hospitalizations, medications, and other matters relating to your health. The patient and family are responsible for reporting unexpected changes in the patient's condition. The patient and the family help the hospital improve its understanding of the patient's environment by providing feedback about service needs and expectations.
- Report pain: inform care providers of your level of pain and the effectiveness of provided treatment. Ask questions when you do not understand what you have been told about your care or what you are expected to do.
- Follow instructions: you are responsible for following the care, service or treatment plan developed. You should express any concerns you have about your ability to follow and comply with the proposed care plan or course of treatment. Every effort is made to adapt the plan to your specific needs and limitations. When such adaptations to the treatment plan are not recommended you and your family are responsible for understanding the consequences of the treatment alternatives and not following the proposed course.

- Accept consequences: you and your family are responsible for the outcomes if you do not follow the care, service or treatment plan.
- Follow rules and regulations: you and your family are responsible for following the hospital's rules and regulations concerning patient care and conduct.
- Show respect and consideration: for the hospital's personnel and property, other patients, help control noise and disturbances, and following smoking policies.
- Meet financial commitments: by promptly meeting any financial obligation agreed to with the hospital.

The patient's family or surrogate decision-maker assumes the above responsibility for the patient if the patient has been found by his or her physician to be incapable of understanding these responsibilities, has been judged incompetent in accordance with law, or exhibits a communication barrier.

Reprinted with permission by the author

Sample Medical Information and Privacy Statement

EXAMPLE ONLY.
Each hospital has its own personalized Medical Information and Privacy Statement.
Consult your hospital.

THIS NOTICE DESCRIBES HOW MEDICAL INFORMATION ABOUT YOU MAY BE USED AND DISCLOSED AND HOW YOU CAN GET ACCESS TO THIS INFORMATION. PLEASE REVIEW IT CAREFULLY.

This page provides a brief summary of your privacy rights. Please read Pages 2–6 for a full description of your rights. if you need more information, you may call Patient Relations at ext. XXXX.

This notice describes the privacy practices of the [Sample Hospital], Holding Company and associated doctors, jointly known as [Sample Hospital]. These organizations are allowed to share medical information with each other for treatment, payment, and operational activities. We will use this information in order to provide our patients with complete and comprehensive healthcare services.

OUR COMMITMENT TO YOU

We are committed to protecting your medical information. [Sample Hospital] is required by law to keep medical information about you private, to give you this Notice about our privacy practices and to follow the practices outlined in this Notice.

HOW WE MAY USE AND DISCLOSE YOUR MEDICAL INFORMATION

We may use your medical information for treatment (such as sending medical information about you to your referring physician), payment (such as sending a bill to your insurance company), and for healthcare operations (such as teaching students or evaluating the performance of our staff).

Under certain circumstances we are allowed to use or disclose your medical information without your written permission. We may give out information about you for public health purposes, reports of abuse, neglect, or domestic violence, health oversight audits or inspections, research studies, funeral arrangements and organ donations, government programs, workers' compensation, and emergency situations. We also disclose patient information when required by law, such as in response to a request from law enforcement or in response to judicial orders.

We also may contact you for appointment reminders, to tell you about possible treatment options and health services, or for fundraising efforts. If you are a hospital inpatient, we will put your name in our facility directory unless you tell us otherwise. We may disclose medical information about you to a friend or family member who is involved in your care.

YOUR RIGHTS CONCERNING YOUR MEDICAL INFORMATION

You have the right to inspect or copy your medical information. There may be a fee for this service. You may ask us to amend the medical information you believe is incorrect or incomplete. You may have a list of non-routine disclosures we have made about you. You may request special confidential communications. You may request restrictions on information disclosed about you. You have the right to complain to us and to the federal government if you believe your privacy rights have been violated. You have a right to a paper copy of this notice.

We reserve the right to make changes to this Notice. We will post a copy of the current Notice in the locations where you receive services.

Effective: DATE

THIS NOTICE DESCRIBES HOW MEDICAL INFORMATION ABOUT YOU MAY BE USED AND DISCLOSED AND HOW YOU CAN GET ACCESS TO THIS INFORMATION. PLEASE REVIEW IT CAREFULLY.

If you have any questions about this Notice, please call Patient Relations at XXXX.

WHO WILL FOLLOW THIS NOTICE

This Notice describes the privacy practices of the [Sample Hospital]. [Sample Hospital] is made up of the separate healthcare organizations listed below. To better serve you, [Sample Hospital] jointly provides you with this Notice regarding privacy practices of [Sample Hospital] and your privacy rights established by the Health Insurance Portability and Accountability Act of 1996 (HIPAA). The healthcare organizations that participate in this joint Notice, including their separate sites of services, have each agreed to follow the terms of this Notice as permitted by HIPAA. Upon request, we will provide you with a list of sites and locations of the [Sample Hospital] that apply to this Notice.

The [Sample Hospital] includes the following organizations:

- The [Sample Hospital];
- The hospital holding company;
- All of the affiliated doctors.

The organizations listed above include employees, staff, trainees, volunteer groups, and other healthcare personnel.

These organizations, sites and locations may share your medical information with each other for treatment, payment or healthcare operations purposes described in this Notice and are allowed to do so by law for the benefit of providing you with efficient healthcare services.

IMPORTANT DISCLAIMER

THE ORGANIZATIONS PARTICIPATING IN THIS JOINT NOTICE FOR [SAMPLE HOSPITAL] ARE PARTICIPATING ONLY FOR THE PURPOSES OF PROVIDING THIS JOINT NOTICE AND SHARING HEALTH INFORMATION AS PERMITTED BY APPLICABLE LAW AND ARE NOT IN ANY WAY PROVIDING HEALTHCARE SERVICES MUTUALLY OR ON EACH OTHER'S BEHALF. EACH ORGANIZATION PARTIPATING IN THIS JOINT NOTICE FOR [SAMPLE HOSPITAL] IS AN INDIVIDUAL HEALTHCARE PROVIDER AND EACH IS INDIVIDUALLY RESPONSIBLE FOR ITS OWN ACTIVITIES, INCLUDING

COMPLIANCE WITH PRIVACY LAWS, AND ALL HEALTHCARE SERVICES IT PROVIDES.

OUR PLEDGE REGARDING MEDICAL INFORMATION

We understand that medical information about you and your health is personal. We are committed to protecting medical information about you. We create a record of the care and services you receive at [Sample Hospital]. We need this record to provide you with complete and comprehensive care and to comply with certain legal requirements. This Notice applies to all of the records your care generates at [Sample Hospital].

This Notice tells you about the ways in which we may use and disclose medical information about you. It also describes your rights and certain obligations we have regarding the use and disclosure of medical information.

We are required by law to:

- make sure that medical information that identifies you is kept private;
- give you this Notice of our legal duties and privacy practices with respect to medical information about you; and
- follow the terms of this Notice currently in effect.

HOW WE MAY USE AND DISCLOSE MEDICAL INFORMATION ABOUT YOU

The following categories describe different ways that we use and disclose medical information. Not every use or disclosure in a category will be listed. However, all of the ways we are permitted to use and disclose information will fall within one of these categories.

1. <u>For Treatment</u>. We may use medical information about you to provide you with medical treatment or services. We may disclose medical information about you to doctors, nurses, technicians, students, or other [Sample Hospital] personnel. For example, different departments of [Sample Hospital] may share medical information about you in order to coordinate elements of your care, such as prescriptions, lab work and x-rays. We also may disclose medical information about you to people outside [Sample Hospital] such as referring physicians and home healthcare nurses in connection with your healthcare treatment.
2. <u>For Payment</u>. We may use and disclose medical information about you to your insurance plan, or other parties who help pay for your care. For example, we may tell your health plan about a treatment you are going to

receive to determine whether your plan will pay for that treatment.

3. <u>For Heath Care 0perations</u>. We may use and disclose medical information about you for [Sample Hospital] operations. These uses and disclosures are necessary to run [Sample Hospital] and to make sure that all of our patients receive quality care. For example, we may use medical information to review our treatment and services and to evaluate the performance of our staff in caring for you. We may also disclose information to doctors, nurses, technicians, students, and other healthcare personnel for teaching purposes.

4. <u>Business Associates</u>. There may be some activities provided for our organization through contracts with outside businesses. Examples include transcription services and collection agencies. Under such contracts, we may disclose your health information to these businesses to perform the job we have asked them to do. These contracts also require businesses to protect the health information we disclose to them.

5. <u>Appointment Reminders</u>. We may contact you to remind you about your appointment for medical care.

6. <u>Treatment Alternatives</u>. We may use and disclose medical information to tell you about possible treatment

options or alternatives that may be of interest to you and other health related benefits and services.

7. Hospital Directory. We may include certain limited information about you in the hospital directory while you are an inpatient at the hospital. This information may include your name, location in the hospital, your general condition (fair, stable, etc.) and your religious affiliation. The directory information, except for your religious information, may also be disclosed to people who ask for you by name. Your religious affiliation may be given to a member of the clergy, even if they don't ask for you by name. We provide this service so your family, friends and clergy can visit you in the hospital and generally know how you are doing. If you are admitted to the hospital, we will not provide this information or even acknowledge your presence in the Hospital at your request. Contact the Admitting Department at XXX-XXX-XXXX if you do not want this information provided.

8. Individuals Involved In Your Care. Unless you object, we may disclose medical information about you to a friend or family member who is involved in your medical care and we may disclose medical information about you to an entity assisting in a disaster relief effort so that your family can be notified about your location and condition.

If you are not present or able to object, then we may, using our professional judgment, determine whether the disclosure is in your best interest.

9. <u>Research</u>. As an academic medical center, we may use and disclose medical information about you for research purposes. We will only use and disclose your information for a research project if we obtain your permission, or if the need to obtain your permission has been waived by a designated review committee that meets Federal requirements.

10. <u>As Required by Law</u>. We will disclose medical information about you when required to do so by federal, state or local law.

11. <u>Fundraising Activities</u>. We may use information about you to contact you in an effort to raise funds for [Sample Hospital] and its operations. We may disclose information about you to a foundation related to [Sample Hospital] so that the foundation may contact you in raising funds, including, for example, mailing you invitations to fundraising events, mailing you annual financial reports, and other types of mailings related to fundraising activities. We would only disclose contact information, such as your name, address and phone number and the dates you received treatment or services. If you do not wish to be contacted for [Sample Hospital] fundraising

purposes, contact [Sample Hospital] Endowment at ext. XXXX.

12. <u>To Avert A Serious Threat to Health or Safety</u>. We may use and disclose medical information about you when necessary to prevent a serious threat to your health and safety or the health and safety of others. Disclosure would only be to persons who could help prevent the threat.

HOW WE MAY USE AND DISCLOSE MEDICAL INFORMATION ABOUT YOU–SPECIAL SITUATIONS

1. <u>Organ and Tissue Donation</u>. We may disclose medical information to organizations that handle and monitor organ donation and transplantation.

2. <u>Military</u>. If you are a member of the armed forces, we may disclose medical information about you as required by military command authorities. We may also disclose medical information about foreign military personnel to the appropriate foreign military authority.

3. <u>Workers Compensation</u>. We may disclose medical information about you for workers' compensation or similar programs to the extent necessary to comply with laws relating to workers' compensation or other similar

programs established by law. These programs provide benefits for work-related injuries or illness.

4. <u>Public Heath Risks.</u> As required by law, we may disclose medical information about you for public health activities. For example, we may undertake these activities:
   a. to prevent or control disease, injury or disability;
   b. to report births and deaths;
   c. to report child abuse or neglect;
   d. to report reactions to medications or problems with products;
   e. to notify people of recalls of products they may be using;
   f. to notify a person who may have been exposed to a disease or may be at risk for contracting or spreading a disease or condition; and
   g. to notify the appropriate government authority if we believe a patient has been the victim of abuse, neglect or domestic violence. We will only make this disclosure subject to certain requirements when mandated or authorized by law.

5. <u>Health Oversight Activities and Registries</u>. We may disclose medical information to a health oversight agency for activities authorized by law and to patient registries for conditions such as tumor, trauma and burn.

These oversight activities include, for example, audits, investigations, inspections and licensure surveys. These activities are necessary for the government to monitor the healthcare system, the outbreak of disease, government programs, compliance with civil rights laws, and to improve patent outcomes.

6. <u>Lawsuits and Disputes</u>. If you are involved in a lawsuit or a dispute, we may disclose medical information about you in response to a court or administrative order. We may also disclose medical information about you in response to a subpoena, discovery request, or other lawful process.

7. <u>Law Enforcement. We may disclose medical information if asked to do so by a law enforcement official:</u>
   a. for the reporting of certain types of wounds;
   b. in response to a court order, subpoena, warrant, summons or similar process;
   c. to identify or locate a suspect, fugitive, material witness, or missing person;
   d. about the victim of a crime, if under certain limited circumstances, we are unable to obtain the person's agreement;
   e. about a death we believe may be the result of criminal conduct;

f. about suspected criminal conduct on the premises; and

g. in emergency circumstances to report a crime; the location of the crime or victims; or the identity, description or location of the person who committed the crime.

8. <u>Coroners, Medical Examiners and Funeral Directors</u>. We may disclose medical information to a coroner or medical examiner. This may be necessary, for example, to identify a deceased person or determine the cause of death. We may also disclose medical information about patients of the hospital to funeral directors as necessary to carry out their duties.

9. <u>National Security</u>. We may disclose medical information about you to authorized federal officials for purposes of national security.

10. <u>Inmates</u>. An inmate does not have the right to this Notice.

YOUR RIGHTS REGARDING MEDICAL INFORMATION ABOUT YOU

You have the following rights regarding medical information we maintain about you:

1. <u>Right To Inspect and Copy</u>. You have the right to inspect and have copied medical information used to make decisions about your care. Usually, this includes medical and billing records, but does not include some records such as psychotherapy notes. To inspect and have copied medical information used to make decisions about you, you must submit your request in writing. Call Release of Information at XXXX for further details. We may charge a fee for the costs of processing your request. Under very limited circumstances, your request may be denied, such as a request for psychotherapy notes. You may request that a denial be reviewed by contacting Patient Relations at ext. XXXX.

2. <u>Right To Amend</u>. If you feel that medical information we have about you is incorrect or incomplete, you may ask us to amend the information. You have the right to request an amendment of your record for as long as the information is kept by or for [Sample Hospital]. To request an amendment to your record, your request must be made in writing and submitted to the Director of Medical Records. address. In addition, you must provide a reason that supports your request. We may deny your request for an amendment to your record if it is not in writing or does not include a reason to support

the request. We also may deny your request if you ask us to amend information that:

a. was not created by us, unless the person or entity that created the information is no longer available to make the amendment;

b. is not part of the records used to make decisions about you;

c. is not part of the information which you are permitted to inspect and copy; or

d. is accurate and complete.

3. <u>Right To an Accounting of Disclosures</u>. You have the right to receive a list of the disclosures we made of your medical information. This list will not include all disclosures made. For example, this list will not include disclosures we made for treatment, payment, healthcare operations, disclosures made prior to [Month, Day, Year], or disclosures you specifically authorized. To request this list or 'account of disclosures', you must submit your request in writing on the authorized form [Sample Hospital] will provide to you upon request.

4. <u>Right To Request Restrictions</u>. You have the right to request a restriction or limitation on the medical information we use or disclose about you for treatment, payment or healthcare operations. You also have the right to request a limit on the medical information

we disclose about you to someone who is involved in your care or in the payment for your care, like a family member or friend. We are not required to agree to your request. If we do agree, we will comply with your request unless the information is needed to provide you emergency treatment. To request restrictions, you must make your request in writing on a form that will be provided to you, upon your request. You must tell us: (1) what information you want to limit, (2) whether you want to limit our use, disclosure or both, and (3) to whom you want the limits to apply.

5. <u>Right To A Paper Copy of This Notice</u>. You may ask us to give you a copy of this Notice at anytime. Even if you have agreed to receive this Notice electronically, you are still entitled to a paper copy of this notice.

REVISIONS TO THIS NOTICE

We may revise this Notice to reflect any changes in our privacy practices. We reserve the right to make the revised or changed Notice effective for medical information we already have about you as well as for any information we receive in the future. We will post a copy of the current Notice in the locations where you receive services. The effective date of this notice is found on the first page, in the top right hand corner.

COMPLAINTS

If you believe your privacy rights have been violated, you may file a complaint with [Sample Hospital] or with the Secretary of the Department of Health and Human Services. To file a complaint with [Sample Hospital], contact the Privacy Officials of [Sample Hospital], through the office of Patient Relations at ext. XXXX. You will not be penalized for filing a complaint.

OTHER USES OF MEDICAL INFORMATION

Other uses and disclosures of medical information not covered by this Notice or by other laws that apply to us will be made only with your written authorization. If you provide authorization to use or disclose medical information about you, you may revoke that authorization, in writing, at anytime. If you revoke your authorization, we will no longer use or disclose medical information about you for the reasons covered by your written authorization. We are unable to take back any disclosures we have already made with your authorization, and we are required to retain records of the care that we provided to you.

Actively Participate in the Billing/Payment Process

Tons of mistakes are made here, mistakes you will ultimately pay for if you fail to exercise close oversight.

The Patient Advocacy Statement includes a section called Patient Responsibilities. I find it interesting there is no corresponding section called Hospital Responsibilities. Two Patient Responsibilities merit special examination.

Patient Responsibilities

- *Follow rules and regulations: you and your family are responsible for following the hospital's rules and regulations concerning patient care and conduct.*
We are told to follow the rules, many times without even knowing what they are.

- *Meet financial commitments: by promptly meeting any financial obligation agreed to with the hospital.*
We are told to "pay our bills," even in the absence of documentation directly from the provider. This is inevitably going to give you gastrointestinal problems, but you need to know about it. All of the hospitals we experienced used the type of accounting that is easiest for them. Bill calls it the "revolving charge" method, borrowed from the credit card companies. The following

is a portion of one of our actual statements. I have reproduced it here to illustrate:

1. What bills typically look like, and
2. How important (and confusing!) it is to review each bill/statement carefully.

HOSPITAL NAME		STATEMENT DATE	
HOSPITAL CONTACT INFO		ACCOUNT NO.	
		PATIENT NAME	
		MEDICAL RECORD NO.	
		AMOUNT DUE	
MO DY YR	**Provider/Description of Services**	**Billed to Insurance**	**Personal Balance**
	The following services were provided by: NAME OF DOCTOR		
1/13/2001	PLACEMENT OF DRAINS, PERI — #1		770.00 — #3
1/13/2001	ARTERIAL LINE PERCUTANEOUS		225.00 — #3
1/13/2001	INSERT CENT VEN CATH PERC		251.00 — #3
1/13/2001	BLOOD GASES		250.00 — #3
1/13/2001	ANESTHESIA COMP BY EMERGE		110.00 — #3
2/20/2001	PMT–Name of Insurance Co,		-456.20 — #4
2/20/2001	ADJUSTMENT		-1065.75— #5
3/09/2001	PMT ON ACCT/AUTO CBO CHEC		-114.05 — #6
4/03/2001	INSERT CENT VEN CATH PERC — #2	251.00 — #2	
6/27/2001	UNLISTED PROCEDURE, VASC	330.00 — #7	

Steps in billing (numbers correspond with steps):

1. Hospital/Doctor provides service
2. Hospital/Doctor bills insurance company for service. Amount is placed in "Billed to Insurance" column.
3. At some point, the Hospital/Doctor determines insurance has either paid all they are going to pay or, in the absence of any payment, the individual is responsible for the bill. The fee for the service then moves to the "Personal Balance" column.
4. Insurance pays and forwards an Explanation of Benefits (EOB) to Hospital/Doctor and Patient (Insured).
5. Insurance deducts amount of bill agreed upon between Hospital/Doctor and Insurance Company (when Hospital/Doctor agreed to become a "Preferred Provider").
6. Unknown payment to account.
7. Unknown procedure done that may, justifiably, result in refusal to pay by Insurance Company.

Without getting into the "ethics" of billing, let's look at what is wrong with this bill, step by step (number by number):

1. The name of the service provided is abbreviated and technical jargon is used so lay people rarely understand it.

2. The charge sent to the insurance company is frequently positioned nowhere close to the actual charge on the bill. Sometimes they are on different pages. As a result, you have to hunt and cross-check to ensure all charges have been submitted to insurance.
3. Apparently, the first five items on this bill had previously been submitted to insurance for payment. I cannot be sure unless I check prior bills received from this provider and look for the same charges in the "Billed to Insurance" column. In any case, I don't know:
   a. if the provider has actually received a "Determination of Benefits" statement from my insurance carrier (again without matching this bill up with the carrier's "Explanation of Benefits"); OR
   b. if the provider has simply decided the insurance company has had enough time to process this change and is now moving on to attempt full collection from the patient.
4. The provider actually did receive money from the insurance company as indicated by the minus sign. Can you tell what the payment was for? I can't. The only possible solution here is again for me to go back to the "Explanation of Benefits" from the insurance company and try to match the credit up with a payment made by them. The problem with this is each "Explanation of

Benefits" includes multiple listings/payments and the provider may have added up several charges, in order to reach the credit amount, making it all but impossible to know which ones are involved.

5. This is an amount of money the hospital will never collect and they "write it off" as the cost of participating in this insurance carrier's plan. Again, there may be multiples.

6. I am clueless (as apparently is the provider) as to where and from whom the payment under this entry came. It wasn't from us but far be it from me to dispute any credit! However, there is a chance this may be removed at some future point and since you don't know where the money came from, you can't dispute its removal.

7. This is a **guaranteed** insurance collection problem as the specific nature of the procedure was not coded correctly. All we know is that some sort of procedure was conducted by "vascular." Therefore, the insurance company will deny benefits. As a result, rather than correct the coding, this provider moved the charge to the "Personal Balance" column in a subsequent bill and sent it to an outside collection agency that harassed us for payment.

With the help of our insurance carrier, we specified that no payment would be forthcoming from either insurance or the Bucks until specific documentation was provided. The collections agency stated that providers are often more willing to provide them with the documentation than the patient or insurance companies, since they want their money! What is wrong with this picture? We are presently in collections with five agencies (for as little as $84) because documentation was either erroneous or not forthcoming. This, after our respective insurance companies have paid out approximately $1.75 million in claims!

The purpose of the previous discussion is not to get you worried about bills and collections agencies. Deal with these issues as they arise. Perhaps your relationships will go more smoothly than ours did. There are two things to commit to memory from this example:

- Challenge anything that does not look right to you! Ask for clarification and additional documentation. You have the right to require the hospital to detail every expense associated with every service. Make the providers and insurance carriers live up to their obligations, even though Patient Rights Statements are silent about exactly what those obligations are; and

- If you cannot understand or do not wish to spend your energy dealing with your bills, insurance forms, or payment records, get help! Help is available from many sources.

After months of dealing with entry-level clerks at the insurance company, who could only say what they had been told to say and, frankly, made many mistakes, I finally **insisted** (this is part of your advocacy) on speaking with a supervisor. It took five attempts to finally be passed to one, but we ultimately became friends with her! She saved us thousands of dollars in mistakes and advocated on our behalf when there were problems with interpretations and partner companies.

We also had our brother-in-law (who is an accountant) helping us with our bills for a while during Bill's hospitalization when my full attention was on Bill.

Ultimately, we required the help of Bill's employer to "strong arm" a former reluctant insurance provider, who failed to provide the agreed-upon service after they were dropped as the insurance company for Bill's employer.

Save all your statements and light a bonfire when you are certain that payouts and medical obligation payments are behind you. And, most of all, remember—you are not alone!

Additional Resources

Visit http://www.24-7ordead.com for terminology, information and continuously updated tools and sources of assistance for patient advocacy.

Printed in the United States
42557LVS00005B/115-408